Enjoy the Journey

Building Wealth

Elaine & Scott Manley

FINANCIAL JOURNEY PARTNERS®
Partners in Your Financial Journey®

For more copies or information, contact us at FinancialJourney.com

Printed in the United States

ISBN eBook: 979-8-9892056-6-0
ISBN Paperback: 979-8-9892056-7-7
ISBN Hardcover: 979-8-9892056-8-4
Library of Congress Control Number: 2025917721

Disclosures

The information contained in this book is intended to provide general information for educational purposes only, as investment recommendations and decisions must consider your specific facts and circumstances. This material should not be construed as an offer of, or recommendation of, any security, nor should it be construed as offering investment advice, nor be viewed as an advertisement for advisory services.

The stories are of actual clients of Financial Journey Partners. Clients were not compensated with cash or non-cash in any way for their statements. We are not aware of any material conflicts of interest. The views expressed are those of the authors and do not necessarily reflect the views of Mutual Advisors, LLC, or Mutual Securities, Inc., or any of its affiliates.

Financial Journey Partners Logo, Partners in Your Financial Journey, and FJP Retirement Framework are registered trademarks of Financial Journey Partners, Inc. Any unauthorized use is expressly prohibited.

Certified Financial Planner Board of Standards, Inc. (CFP Board) owns the CFP® certification mark, the CERTIFIED FINANCIAL PLANNER™ certification mark, and the CFP® certification mark (with plaque design) logo in the United States, which it authorizes use of by individuals who successfully complete CFP Board's initial and ongoing certification requirements.

CA Insurance License for Elaine Manley - 0706550
CA Insurance License for Scott Manley - 0C96859

Contents

Introduction

We have observed that the knowledge to be financially successful and to build wealth between the ages of 25 to 55 is not taught adequately in high school or college. It is not taught in most jobs. There are books that address specific financial topics, without providing a comprehensive picture of all that is involved with creating a comprehensive financial plan. This book was written to provide education on the significant financial topics for a person to consider between the ages of 25 to 55. This book will give you a framework to pull together the important and essential elements.

Many times, our older clients have said to us:
"I wish I had started saving when I was younger."
"I wish I knew what I know now when I was younger."
"I wish I had started working with a financial advisor when I was younger."

People say these things because they often learn by trial and error, without the experience and wisdom to make optimal decisions. We want to pass on the knowledge and wisdom we have obtained from decades of experience of wealth management planning. As you will see throughout this book, our clients are also willing to share some of their experiences. We want you to benefit from the learnings of people who have successfully navigated their journey.

We are Elaine and Scott Manley, Wealth Managers, and the authors of this book. We created the firm, Financial Journey Partners, to help families reach their financial goals. We have decades of experience helping our clients and their adult kids. We have advised them through all the phases of their life, from taking their first full-time job through the end of their life. If you are between the ages of 25 to 55, this book is specifically written to help you think through your important financial and life decisions in an organized and structured way. We will explain a structured process with the essential elements for you to consider when planning your financial future. We want to help you make the best decisions for you.

In this book, we will share stories from clients who have been successful. They are people who have made smart decisions with their finances. We call them "Real Client Stories". They are meant to be a guide for you, to be inspirational, and to help you learn from others who have been successful. We have also included an exercise at the end of each chapter to help you think through the important questions in the chapter.

As Wealth Managers, we help people reach their financial goals. Our decades of experience helping people of all ages gives us the knowledge needed to assist people as they reach the milestones in their life. We have seen many individuals work their entire lives to reach the point where they are financially independent and no longer need to work. This provides great joy and satisfaction as they move into retirement. Sadly, a few people have reached this point, only to suffer a medical illness or pass away without ever getting to do many of the things they had dreamed of accomplishing.

We think it's important for people of all ages to *Enjoy the Journey* throughout their entire working career and during retirement. We feel so passionate about this that we put a sign on our office wall, right as you walk in our front door, that says: "*Enjoy the Journey.*" In addition to helping people of all ages, we are committed to living our lives this way and helping our team and family *Enjoy the Journey*.

This book is designed to be practical and inspirational. It will help you make smart decisions as you *Enjoy the Journey*. Now, let's begin your journey.

Exercise:

What Is Unique About My Situation?

Instructions: Each person's situation is unique. Your goals and concerns will likely change at different stages of your life. List the things about your situation, at this stage in your life, that you think are unique to you and your specific situation. List the barriers to your current financial situation that you must overcome and opportunities to improve your situation.

What makes my financial situation unique?

Barriers to Overcome?

Opportunities to Include?

1: Mistakes to Avoid

As a person moves through their life from ages 25 to 55, many major life events can occur that result in significant life changes. These may include:

- getting a first full-time job,
- getting married,
- buying a house,
- having children,
- changing careers,
- paying for college education for your children, and
- saving for retirement.

Navigating through these years with all these life changes can be very challenging. These events may result in conflicting priorities that are competing for the limited financial resources that are available. These years can leave people feeling stretched financially, resulting in confusion and stress. An ideal time to start developing a financial plan is when you get your first full-time job.

When people finish their schooling (high school or college) and start their first full-time job, most people have little or no savings. Even worse, after college, some people we have met have little savings and large student loans. In contrast, when people reach their 50s, their financial situation may be significantly different. Often, student loans are paid off. They had time to pay down their debt, and they have accumulated significant savings and investments.

Individuals in this period have frequently been labeled as part of the "sandwich generation". By the time they reach their 50s, they may find themselves with conflicting priorities from the goals for themselves, their kids, and their aging parents. There may not be enough time and money to care for the financial needs of three generations. What is the best way to make smart decisions over the 30 years from ages 25 to 55, and to build the wealth necessary to achieve all your goals? We are going to discuss it in this book.

When we first talk with individuals between the ages of 25 to 55, we often see people making a range of mistakes that can significantly challenge them from reaching their goals. Let's discuss some of the common mistakes that we have seen.

EMERGENCY RESERVE IS TOO SMALL, OR NOT AT ALL

It is very important to have an emergency reserve to be able to cover unexpected expenses. These can come from a range of events. Here are some of the more common, unfortunate ones we see:

- getting laid off and losing your job,
- major car repair,
- car accident requiring the replacement of your car,

- paying for medical bills, and
- lost income when missing workdays due to an illness.

During unfortunate events, a lack of an adequate emergency reserve can add significant stress to an already difficult situation. We have seen people take money out of their retirement accounts when there is not enough in emergency reserves to handle a short-term crisis. Taking money out of retirement accounts before 59 ½ can result in the loss of up to 50 percent, due to federal taxes, state taxes, and penalties. Having an adequate emergency reserve is very important. We will discuss this more in Chapter 4.

SPENDING TOO MUCH

One might think that people who have higher incomes tend to save more money. This is not always the case. We have seen people who make less money save more than people with much larger salaries, simply because they control their spending and are able to save more. We believe it is important to create a budget that includes how much you can spend and how much to save to meet your financial goals. A very successful way to limit spending and maximize savings may be to live at home with your parents for the first few years of your working career.

From our experience, many people in the working part of their career want freedom and flexibility to spend as much as they want on whatever they want. This can lead to spending more than is really needed and saving less than is required to fund all your financial goals. We encourage you to create a budget, monitor your spending, and be intentional about how you spend your hard-earned money. Software programs are available to make it easier to track and categorize your spending.

An important part of creating a budget is setting goals for how much you will save. This should include saving money into your retirement plan at work, if one is offered by your employer. We will talk more about that in Chapter 5.

WAITING TOO LONG TO START SAVING FOR RETIREMENT

When a person is in their 20s, retirement can seem too far away to care. In these early working years, there can be many short-term demands for money, including:

- creating an emergency reserve,
- paying off student loans,
- furnishing a first apartment,
- saving for a wedding ring, and
- paying for a wedding and honeymoon.

We have seen some people delay saving for their retirement for 5, 10, 15 years or longer after they started working.

Getting a late start saving for retirement can result in a person needing to work much longer than they want. We strongly encourage people to begin saving money into a retirement account as soon as they start working in a full-time job. The most common method for saving for retirement is to save in a retirement account if it is offered through your employer. We will discuss this more in Chapter 5.

INVESTING WITH TOO LITTLE OR TOO MUCH RISK

We have seen people take too much risk with their stock investments and lose a large part of their savings and investments. There have been periods where the U.S. stock market has lost 35 to 50 percent. This includes the Dotcom crash of 2000-2002, the Great Financial Crisis of 2008-2009, COVID Pandemic in 2020, and the Inflation and Interest Rate Spike of 2022. While the stock market came back to reach all-time highs after each period above, it can be very uncomfortable watching your savings go down considerably during these periods.

We have also seen people put all their extra money into checking and savings accounts in the bank that have little or no return. They are missing the potential growth of their savings from a diversified portfolio in the stock market.

SINGLE STOCK RISK

Some companies have programs for employees to purchase the stock of their company at a discount. Buying company stock regularly and holding it over many years has worked very well for people who worked for some of the largest tech companies. On the other hand, we have also seen people buy stock in small start-up companies. In some cases, the stock of the small company has gone up and then crashed, causing people to lose millions of dollars. We will talk about this more in Chapter 5. The important point here is that the strategy for holding a large amount of company stock can be very risky.

There are also a lot of examples where companies saw their stock value soar when the company was growing and doing well. There have been companies that lost their way, have had a difficult time and their stock value plummets. We believe that if a person is going to own individual stock, it is important to review the holdings regularly and be ready to sell stocks if they start doing poorly. We like to say, “Love your spouse and love your children. Don't love your stocks". We will discuss strategies for saving for your future in Chapter 5.

NO LIFE INSURANCE

We sometimes see individuals aged 25 to 55 with no life insurance, not enough life insurance, or the wrong type of life insurance. An important milestone that often gets parents thinking about life insurance is the birth of their first kid. The appropriate type and amount of life insurance can ensure the goals of both parents are completed, even if one or both parents pass at a young age. These goals include living in the family home until the kids are done with college and paying for their education.

When a couple purchases their first home, a goal of the couple may be to ensure that their family can live in this home until all the kids are done with college. Having enough life insurance on both parents to pay off the mortgage may be appropriate in this situation. We will review the different types of life insurance and how to select the correct amount for your situation in Chapter 6.

PARENTS PAY FOR COLLEGE EDUCATION BEYOND WHAT THEY CAN AFFORD

Parents often want to see their kids graduate from high school and continue their education to get a college degree. A person with a college degree may have the opportunity for higher-paying jobs than a person without a college degree.

We have seen parents get into financial trouble when they think they need to pay the full amount for tuition, housing, and expenses for all their kids to go away to college at a four-year university. Not all parents can afford to do this. We have seen parents take on hundreds of thousands of dollars of debt for their kids' college education in the years just before they were planning to retire. When this happens, these parents are put in a situation where they may need to work much longer than they want and retire at an older age so they can pay off all of the accumulated student debt.

There are options for parents to help their kids get through college without the parents financially jeopardizing their retirement plan. We like to say, "There are loans the kids can get for education, but when the time comes to retire, there are no loans the parents can get to fund their retirement." We will discuss this more in Chapter 7.

NO ESTATE PLAN

Not having an estate plan is a common mistake among individuals and couples aged 25 to 55. This can cause significant problems and large unnecessary expenses.

When a person is 25 and just getting out of college with few assets, an estate plan is likely not a top priority. As a person gets older, life events can make it very important to have an estate plan in place. An estate plan includes several documents that describe how your money and things you own (assets) will be transferred to your beneficiaries after you pass. This would include instructions so that in the event of your passing, you determine who would receive your home and who would raise your kids. With no estate plan, a judge in a Probate Court will make these important decisions for you which ends up costing thousands of dollars and years of wasted time. We will talk more about this in Chapter 8.

NO FINANCIAL PLAN

For most people, when they start working with us, it is the first time they have completed a financial plan of any kind. Until this point, they have been "winging it", perhaps doing some things well and some things not so well. In most cases, those people could be making better decisions to optimize their financial future.

You can create a financial plan on your own. If your situation is very simple, that may be adequate. As people age from 25 to 55, it is likely that their situation will become more complex. Hopefully, their assets will grow, making sound financial decisions become more and more important. If you are creating your own financial plan, we encourage you to do research in this area so you can make smart financial decisions. If you want help, find a financial professional you trust who can guide you to create a personalized financial plan specific to your situation. We will discuss creating a plan for success in Chapter 9.

What are the effects of making one or more of the mistakes above? Making these kinds of mistakes may prevent a person from achieving their financial goals, such as sending their kids to the college of their choice. The result from making these mistakes often requires a person to work longer than they desired and delay their retirement date.

We believe that if a person wants to be successful, they should have clearly defined goals. This includes goals for the short and long term. For example, if one of your goals is to retire, at what age do you ideally want that to happen? We encourage you to think about the most important goals of your life and get them clearly defined, with target completion dates. We will discuss more about setting goals in Chapter 2.

We encourage people to start with the end in mind. Develop your clearly defined goals with target dates and create a plan to get from now to completing your goal. When we say, “Start with the end in mind”, this is what we mean.

A lot of life happens for people between the ages of 25 to 55. This is the bulk of a person’s working career. This is when a person may accumulate much of their wealth. The goals of a person may change considerably during this time frame.

From age 25 to 35, typical goals may include getting a first full-time job, creating an emergency reserve, buying a wedding ring, buying a car, paying for a wedding, moving into your first apartment, having kids, and starting a retirement savings account. From age 35 to 45, typical goals may include purchasing a home, getting life insurance, continuing to save for college education, retirement and paying for memorable family vacations. From age 45 to 55, typical goals may include sending the kids to college, taking advantage of all your work experience to get the most out of your job, and saving more for your retirement.

An important point here is that from age 25 to 55, your goals are likely to change. The relative importance of your different goals will change over time. We believe it is important that you have a comprehensive financial plan to guide you. Your plan should consider these changing priorities and goals over these decades. You may find many conflicting priorities for your hard-earned money. By getting clear on your goals, that should help you make smart decisions that align your money with your objectives.

As we prepared to write this book, we did research by conducting a survey of people in the age range of 25 to 55. We asked them questions related to money and their finances. The feedback we received was consistent with what we have heard from our clients over the past decades. We will share the results of the survey throughout this book.

The first question we asked was, “What is my biggest concern about building wealth before my retirement?” We asked this as an open-ended question rather than selecting from a list of answers, because we did not want to constrain the possible answers. We wanted to give the people answering the survey complete flexibility to answer the question in any way they choose.

By far, the most common answer was some variation of not having enough money to meet their goals. This included:

- not having enough money for retirement,
- not having enough money to live comfortably when retired,
- having investments last long enough, and
- having enough money with the increasingly high cost of living.

A far fewer number of answers were about the mechanics and process of how to build enough wealth to have the money required to meet their goals.

Q1: *What is my biggest concern about building wealth before my retirement?*

We want to give people the confidence that they will have enough money for the rest of their lives. From our experience, we have found the best way to accomplish this is to clearly define their goals and then create a financial plan that identifies the specific steps to take to reach their goals. We will discuss creating a plan for success in Chapter 9.

If you are between the ages of 25 to 55, we wrote this book for you. We want to help you build wealth by making smart decisions that align your money with your goals. For decades, we have been helping people of all ages reach their financial goals. Our experience has shown us that many people ages 25 to 55 are not getting the proper advice and financial education they need to help them make smart financial decisions.

At this point, you might be wondering, "How can I build wealth for myself and my family?" Our experience has shown us that:

"The secret to building wealth over time is to spend less than you make, mitigate taxes, and invest the difference wisely."

- Elaine & Scott Manley

Your next question may be, "How can I build wealth based on my situation?" We want to share a process you can follow to help make this happen.

We understand that during the ages of 25 to 55, trying to achieve all these conflicting goals with a limited amount of money can be confusing and difficult. To help you pull all this together in an organized manner, we created the **FJP Building Wealth Framework™**.

FJP Building Wealth Framework™

Our FJP Building Wealth Framework™ is a structured process to work through all the important elements of your financial plan. It includes the elements we believe are essential for building wealth. This process starts by identifying your values and goals. We designed this process to help you make smart decisions and align your money with your goals so you can Enjoy the Journey. We will explain and discuss this process in detail in Chapter 3.

At first glance, each part of this process should seem like common sense. An important point about this process is that all the elements are considered and included in your plan. You might have some elements working really well, yet missing just one component can still cause big problems or stop you from reaching your goals. The important point is to consider all these elements when creating your financial plan, as it may only be as good as the weakest link.

To help guide you on your journey and reach your goals, we think it is important to think about your core values as they relate to money. Why is this so important? Because our values drive everything we do in life. They have a profound impact on the decisions we make. Our values are very important, yet people may not have thought much about them in relation to their retirement goals.

You may ask yourself profound questions.

- Why am I here on this earth?
- What is my purpose in life?
- What do I want to accomplish before the end of my life?
- When I'm gone, and people think about me, what memories of me do I want them to have?

To help you find answers to these questions, it might help you to start with your values. You may not have spent time thinking about your values or how to articulate them. For example, does money provide security or a sense of freedom to do what you want to do? For you to understand this better, let's start by asking the question, "What do I want my money to do for me?"

If your first answer is to have enough money to pay the bills, we want you to think deeper about this. We hear some people say, "I want to maintain my current lifestyle." Others say, "I don't want to run out of money." Thinking about this more, some people tell us that money gives them a feeling of security or financial freedom to do what they choose.

Great! Now ask yourself, why is security or financial freedom important to me? Maybe it's to take care of your family and friends. Now ask again, why? You may think it is because it is your purpose in life or because it gives you happiness. Each person is unique, and their answers are unique.

We encourage you to do this exercise. Ask yourself the question, "What do I want my money to do for me?" After you get an answer, ask the question, "Why is this important to me?" After each answer, keep asking, "Why is this important to me?" Continue this until you find there is no higher purpose or meaning to the question.

People often stop asking "why" before getting to their true core values. If you are married or have a significant other, we encourage you to do this exercise together; this is a very important step. Take plenty of time here because these answers can greatly impact your decisions in the future. Be sure to have this conversation with your significant other and your financial advisor, if you have one.

If you do this exercise at age 30, you may likely have different answers if you do it again at age 40, 50, and beyond. It is an exercise we encourage you to complete multiple times as you grow older and as your situation changes.

REAL CLIENT STORY

Just Get Started!

If it seems like there are a lot of things to do with my finances and it feels overwhelming, where do I start?

Julie is the daughter of a couple who have been our clients for many years, and she is married to Nick. They are in their early 40s and are focused on building successful careers. They began to build wealth and realized that they would benefit from financial planning. This would ensure they are making smart decisions with their money. When talking with their parents, they mentioned that they would like to start creating their financial plan. Their parents recommended they talk with us.

While Julie and Nick were busy building wealth, they lacked a financial plan that clarified their financial goals. We worked with them to create their financial plan. It included all the important elements to help them achieve their goals, including setting their daughter up for a secure future. There were plenty of things to discuss when we got started.

As we started implementing their financial plan, they rolled over their old 401(k) to a Rollover IRA. They also had a significant amount of money sitting in a checking account. This was much more than was needed for emergency reserves, and it was making very little interest. This money was moved to a brokerage account with diversified investments. This decision was consistent with their risk preferences, to allow their money to grow over time.

We provided Julie and Nick with access to a client portal, which is a secure website that allows them to see all their financial information. This allowed them to see all their bank accounts, credit cards, investment accounts and retirement accounts at work, all in one place. The budgeting tool allows them to classify all their checking and credit card accounts by category. It also allows them to track their spending. This enables them to track their progress towards their goals.

Julie recently started working at her first company that awards her stock grants. We discussed the options for this stock. Next, we created a plan to monitor the stock price and sell it to diversify some of the stock when appropriate.

They started a 529 college savings plan for their young daughter, Emily. This college savings account provides the benefit of tax-free growth if the money is used for qualifying education expenses. It also provides an account that grandparents can use to contribute to their granddaughter's education.

Both Julie and Nick have life insurance through their employers. They liked the idea of starting a permanent life insurance policy for Emily while she is still young. The policy selected allows for the cash value to grow inside the policy over Emily's lifetime. When certain conditions are met, some of the cash value inside the policy can be taken out tax-free when needed. The policy they selected also allows the death benefit to be increased seven times over their daughter's lifetime, if her insurance needs grow.

Next, they decided to simplify their charitable donations by opening a Donor Advised Fund. This allows them to make one contribution into the fund and take a tax deduction for the full amount in the current year. This eliminates the need to keep track of each individual small donation. Then, over the next few years, they can make donations to non-profit organizations of their choice. These donations can be done as one-time donations, or they can schedule regular donations monthly or annually.

There is still more work to be done. They plan to work with an estate attorney who will create their estate plan. Their next step is to select an attorney who will also update the estate plan for their parents, so that the estate planning for multiple generations in their family is well coordinated.

Looking back at this experience, Julie told us, "Prior to creating our financial plan, we felt overwhelmed with the number of different tasks and ways to track money in a variety of places. It felt impossible to know our real net worth and the highest leverage actions we could take. Creating our plan and executing on different phases of it in smaller pieces has made everything much more manageable and noticeably beneficial (to both our bottom line and our peace of mind)."

As Nick looked back at this financial planning process, he said, "It has provided us a holistic picture of our finances, as well as a clear path forward for the future." His biggest benefit was "A path forward toward retirement and financial stability for our family." Julie added that this planning helped them "feel secure with the choices we were making about spending, to enjoy life now, while also preparing for eventual (and hopefully early) retirement."

We asked Nick what he would recommend for other people at this similar point in their lives. "If you are fortunate enough to be able to save money, it is well worth your time to have a professional team guiding you to make the right decisions with those savings. Additionally, it takes some of the worry out of how things look in the future."

To others going through a similar stage in their lives, Julie said, "We really can't recommend enough to just getting started. Don't worry about whether you have enough money to start thinking about it, or how hard it might be to corral everything. Working with Financial Journey Partners has made all that easy -- and they do it all without any judgment about what you've done previously or anywhere you might not be knowledgeable. They take time and care to make sure you feel comfortable with and understand any changes that they are recommending, and we can't recommend them enough!"

Exercise:

What Do I Want My Money to Do for Me?

Instructions: This exercise is to help you understand what you want to accomplish before the end of your life. What is important to you, and what do you want your money to do to help you reach your goals? For the questions below, ask why. Then ask why again to see if there is a deeper meaning. Continue asking why until you find that there is no higher meaning or purpose.

What do I want my money to do for me?

____

____

Why?

____

____

Why?

____

____

Why?

____

____

2: What are My Goals? Now Think Bigger!

We hope you completed the exercise from Chapter 1 to clarify what is important about money to you. We think there is significant value in reviewing this question as you move through different parts of your life.

After gaining clarity on your values and what is important to you, now it's time to think about your goals, both short-term and long-term. We're talking about goals in all areas of your life. This includes goals for yourself, your family, your friends, the groups you belong to, your finances, the causes you are passionate about, and all other areas of your life. Your short-term goals are likely to change and evolve as you move through life from age 25 to 55. Your longer-term goals will also likely change over time. You may find that some longer-term goals (for example, to retire at age 65) may remain constant.

We were recently talking with someone in the age range of 25 to 35. Their immediate goals were saving for a wedding ring, arranging and paying for a wedding, and setting up their first apartment. Their biggest worry was, "How can I ever afford to buy a house?"

In the earlier years of your career, buying a house can seem like a daunting and nearly impossible task. The cost for homes in some states, like California, for example, may be too high for many young people. We have seen young people leaving their families behind and moving to lower-cost states to be able to purchase their first home. When buying your first home, the first step is saving for a down payment. That can be difficult when there are so many other demands for money in earlier years, such as buying a wedding ring, paying for a wedding, and setting up an apartment.

Even after the down payment is saved, affording the monthly payment can seem difficult. What we can say from experience is that most people feel uncomfortable and financially stretched when they buy their first home. However, looking back, many people will say that buying a home was one of their best financial investments.

When we talk with people in their early 50s, the issues are normally quite different than people in their younger years. A major issue for families is figuring out how to pay for each of their kids to go away to college for 4 years at a major university. Our point here is that while someone can feel very stressed in their early years thinking about buying their first house, they may be stressed just as much again in later years thinking about paying for the college education of their kids. Having a financial plan with the specific steps to be taken to reach your goals can help relieve some of the stress.

As you move through your working career from age 25 to 55, your goals are likely to change as your personal and family situation changes. We believe it is important to continually update your goals and your financial plan to reflect these changing goals. We want you to make smart decisions that align your money with your goals. It is about creating the correct balance between your financial goals. Good planning will allow you to make progress on all your goals while avoiding over-funding one goal and under-funding another.

Here are some common financial goals, broken down by age range:

Age 25 to 35

- Get a good full-time job
- Buy or lease a first car
- Pay off student loans
- Buy a wedding ring
- Pay for a wedding
- Furnish a first apartment
- Save for the down payment for a home
- Buy a first home
- Save for retirement

Age 35 to 45

- Upgrade to a larger home
- Take the family on regular vacations
- Save for college education for the kids
- Buy a new car
- Identify a car for the kids to drive when they turn 16
- Save for retirement

Age 45 to 55

- Pay for college education for kids
- Take the kids on a bucket list vacation before they go away to college
- Remodel the home before retirement
- Save for retirement
- Take care of your parents

If you find you have a lot of goals competing for your hard-earned money, this is normal. Most people feel this way. With a sound financial plan, you can achieve your goals.

You will find that there are tradeoffs that you will make to put more money towards some goals and less money towards others. We believe it is important for you to understand the impact of these financial decisions because they can have a major impact on your financial situation in your later years. Our experience has shown us that the best way to understand the impact of these financial decisions is to complete a comprehensive financial plan.

The plan should allow you to see the impact of different decisions and scenarios and to see how they play out over decades in your future. We will highlight in this book some of your most important decisions. When possible, we will explain the pros and cons of these important decisions so you can make the best choice for your situation.

We recommend you review your goals at least once per year. Think about shorter-term goals and longer-term goals. Timeframes for your goals can be this month, one year, five years, or the remainder of your life. Elaine and Scott have the family tradition of updating their goals on January 1st of each year. It's a great time to reflect on how much you have accomplished in the past year. Re-evaluate the unfinished goals to see if it makes sense to keep them on your list, delete them, or replace them with something that means even more to you. Be sure to include the more expensive goals in your financial plan. This will help you understand what you can and cannot afford. In our survey, we wanted to find out more about what goals are the most important for people. We asked the question, "What are my top financial goals?" We asked those taking the survey to rank them in order of importance. The choices given for answers are the following.

- Creating an adequate emergency reserve
- Buying a car
- Paying off student loans
- Paying for a wedding ring and wedding
- Buying a house or condo
- Having one or more children
- Saving for the college education of the children
- Saving for retirement
- Taking care of parents

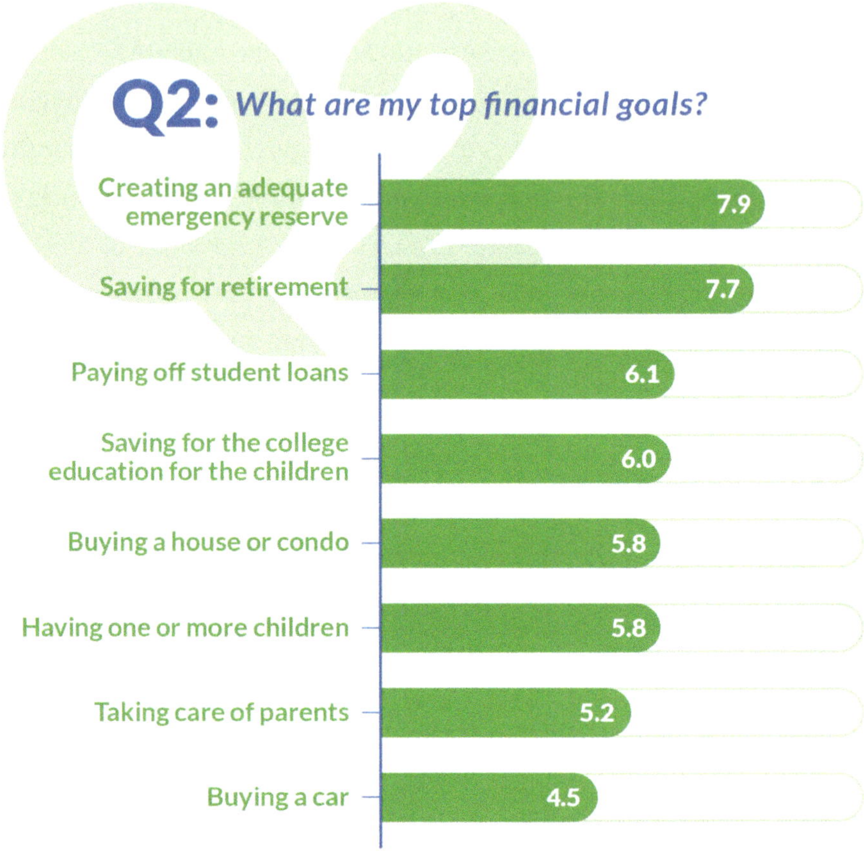

The two answers that were most important were:

- creating an adequate emergency reserve, and
- saving for retirement.

Seeing these as the top two answers, we were wondering how this answer breaks down based on the age ranges of 25-35, 36-45, and 46-55. Here are the percentages of people by age in the survey who chose these as their most important concern.

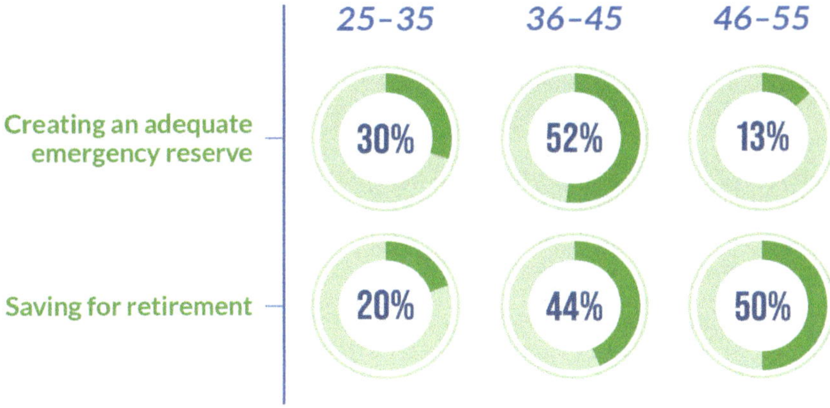

These two financial goals were the top financial goals for most people in our survey. There were several interesting things to note from these numbers.

- 13% of the people aged 46-55 still had creating an emergency reserve as their top financial goal. We encourage people to complete this financial goal as early in life as possible.
- 20% of the people aged 25-35 already have savings for retirement as their top financial goal.

There is no right or wrong answer to the question, "What is your top financial goal?" The answer varies from person to person. Decide what your top financial goal is and create a plan that allows you to achieve your goal.

As you think about your financial goals, this is the time to really open your mind to the possibilities in front of you. It is also the time to think big. We talked with a person recently who said, "I have no clue what my future looks like. It's a good thing because I have a lot of possibilities in front of me." Open your mind to all the exciting possibilities in front of you.

When you have a first draft of your goals, ask yourself, "Can I think bigger?" Then ask yourself, "What would I want as my goals if anything were possible?" If you look at your list of goals and feel excited and inspired, you're on the right track. In the exercise below, it is time to create, define, and refine your goals.

REAL CLIENT STORY

Keep Setting Goals

How do I create a financial plan when family members have different priorities?

Susan has been great at setting goals ever since I met her. She has had a successful career in the tech industry. Throughout her career, she was very good at setting a goal, working on the financial plan on how to accomplish that goal, taking the actions necessary, and achieving the goal. For example, she wanted to buy a house with her husband, Jon. He already owned a small house, however she wanted a bigger home in a nicer neighborhood. Jon was satisfied with what they had and wasn't interested in making the change. Through our discussions, we talked through the pros and cons and what it would take to do this. Susan convinced Jon to proceed, and they created the wealth to make the change.

They have a wonderful son, Owen, who has significant special needs. All of Susan's goals had him in mind every step of the way. She has been able to provide great care and educational solutions as Owen was growing up. Elaine helped Susan and Jon identify the appropriate permanent life insurance and annuity for their situation to achieve the goal of providing for Owen's long-term future. Susan told me, "The peace of mind I find from knowing Owen's future is secure is priceless and the most important goal I have ever achieved."

After many years, Susan decided she'd rather live separately from Jon so she could remain focused on her goals. They all relocated to a new town. She found the home she wanted, and we strategized how to purchase it and make the adjustments she needed to achieve her financial plan. We worked with Jon to create his financial plan which allowed him to meet his goal of being nearby to help with the care for Owen. She then spotted an opportunity to build a new home in a better location, nearby. So, the planning looked at how she could make that happen. With careful budgeting and planning, she was able to build her new home while maintaining her current home. Since then, she has been able to sell her home and move into her new beautiful home. She absolutely loves it, and Jon enjoys being close to his son.

On top of all of this, she was sorting out where her son could live and thrive over the years. Owen was living in a special needs group home that was about an hour from where she currently lived. She set a goal to find a place for her to live near Owen's home. She decided a duplex would be best. Once again, she set the goal, and we used the financial planning tool, along with input from her tax professional, to determine how to best split the cost of the duplex with Jon. They currently rent it out, and eventually she'll move there once she retires. Jon is planning to move into the other unit so both can be close to Owen. This truly shows the dedication to their son and the power of using financial planning for the whole family.

It's a great story of how people can set goals and make them happen. Then look at what more they can do and set that as a goal.

They worked with Elaine, their Wealth Manager, to do a deep analysis of their financial situation. Comprehensive financial planning allowed them to create the best life possible for the entire family.

Exercise:

What Are My Goals? Now Think Bigger!

Instructions: Think about my financial goals and break them down into specific timeframes. What are my goals for:

1. This month

2. This year

3. In five years

4. The rest of my life

3: The FJP Building Wealth Framework™

When you are building wealth during your working career, there are many different financial goals that are competing for your hard-earned money. How do you know what to do first? How do you know how much money to put towards each financial goal? The answers are likely different for each person or couple.

To help you build wealth, we created the FJP Building Wealth Framework™. It is a structured process to work through all the important elements for your financial plan. As Wealth Managers, we have spent decades helping many people from age 25 until the end of their life to be successful. We have decades of experience and understanding to guide people on their financial journey so they can achieve their goals and have a successful retirement. It is exciting to watch people achieve their goals and *Enjoy the Journey*.

The FJP Building Wealth Framework™ includes the elements that our experience has shown are important and essential to help you build wealth and achieve your goals. In this chapter, we will give you an overview of this process and a conceptual explanation of each element.

FJP Building Wealth Framework™

The framework begins with clearly defining your values.

- What is important to me?
- When it comes to your plan for retirement, a good question to ask yourself is "What do I want my money to do for me?
- After you ask yourself this question, then ask yourself, "Why is this important?"

You may need to ask this last question several times to get to your higher purpose or meaning. We discussed this in more detail in Chapter 1, including an exercise to help you clarify your values.

An important part of getting clear on your values is deciding "What relationships matter the most to me?" We encourage you to look at the important people in your life and determine how you want to include them in your life. You may feel that your time is stretched, with not enough time in the day to complete everything. Defining the people who are the most important in your life may help you prioritize where to spend your time.

After gaining clarity on your values and what is important to you, it's now time to think about your goals as far out as you can imagine. We're talking about goals in all areas of your life. This includes goals for yourself, your family, your friends, the groups you belong to, your finances, the causes you are passionate about, and all other areas of your life. When creating your goals, we encourage you to think big and plan big! We discuss this more in Chapter 2, and there is an exercise to help you define your goals.

Now that you have created your goals, it is time to look at your cash flow, create a budget, and determine where you will spend and save your hard-earned money. Without a budget, it is easy to spend money in unplanned ways that may not align with your goals. The first step is to create a budget. Then it is important to track your spending against your budget. The easiest and most efficient way to do this is with an online budgeting tool. It allows you to download all your spending transactions from debit cards, credit cards, and your checking account. There are some excellent online budgeting tools available. We encourage you to find one that works for you. We will discuss this more in Chapter 4.

Part of the process of creating a budget is determining how much money will be allocated to save towards your goals. There are two questions. First is, "How much to save toward each goal?" Second is,

"What is the best way to save for each goal?" Part of your savings plan should be investing your savings in a way that is consistent with your risk level, timeframe, and goals. We will discuss ways to save money and some basic concepts for investing in Chapter 5.

An important part of achieving your goals is to also manage risk if things do not go as planned. Having the correct type and amount of insurance is very important. While there are many books written on different topics related to insurance, we will review some basic concepts about the most common types of insurances in Chapter 6.

If you have kids and intend for them to go to college, that is a huge expense. There are many ways to approach saving for your kid's education. On the low end of cost, kids can live at home and go to a local junior college. On the high end, kids can go away to a university and live away from home for 4 years. The important point here is to select an approach that you can afford, while still achieving your other financial goals. We will discuss this in Chapter 7.

The last element of the FJP Building Wealth Framework™ is estate planning. Estate planning is documenting who receives your assets when you pass away and who will manage that distribution. It includes the creation of Wills, Living Trusts, Power of Attorney documents, Health Care Directives, and other related documents. We believe that estate planning is a very important part of a financial plan. We are surprised by how many people that start working with us have an out-of-date estate plan, or none at all. We have seen people pass away without an estate plan. It is very sad to watch families struggling as their assets go through the probate process, taking years and sometimes costing loved ones thousands of dollars. So please, get an estate plan and make sure it is updated at least once every five years, or as things change. If you move to a new county or state, we recommend you update your estate plan within a year. We will discuss this in Chapter 8.

We were interested to know when the people in our survey would like to retire. We asked the question, "At what age would I like to retire?" The retirement age ranged from 50 to 75. The average age was 61.

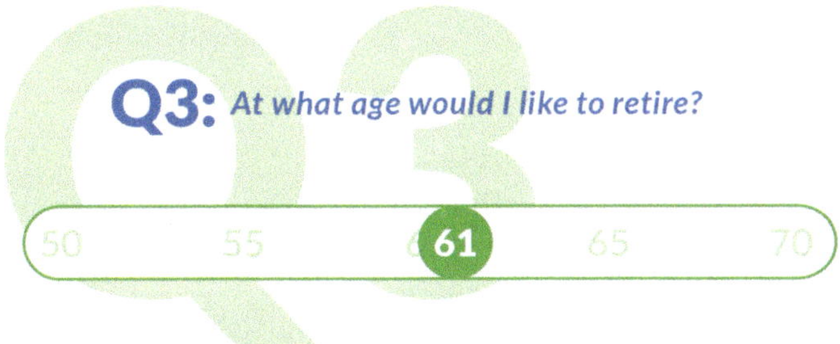

Keep in mind that life expectancy has been increasing over the last decade. If a person retires at age 61, it takes a significant amount of money to maintain the lifestyle they had while they were working.

The next question we asked the people in the survey was, "Based on where I am financially today, at what age do I think I will be able to retire?" The age ranged from 50 to never. The average age was 66.

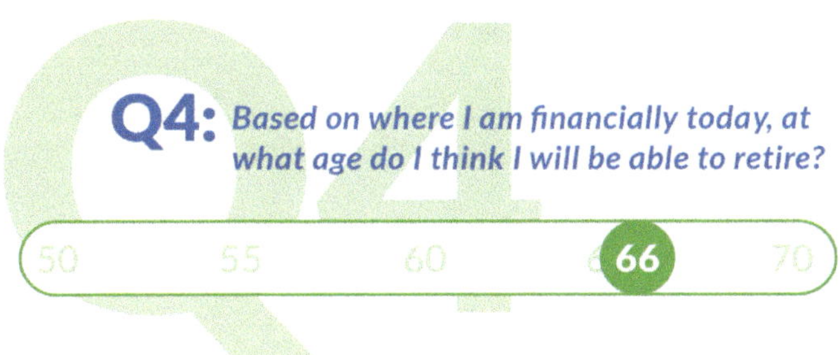

The way to find out if you are on track to retire at your target age is to develop a comprehensive financial plan. If you are not, then a comprehensive financial plan can help you understand what you need to change to get on track to retire at your desired age.

To better understand the concerns the people in the survey have about their retirement, we asked them the question, "When I think about my retirement, what is my top concern?" The top concern for the people in the survey was not being able to continue the lifestyle in retirement that they had while they were working.

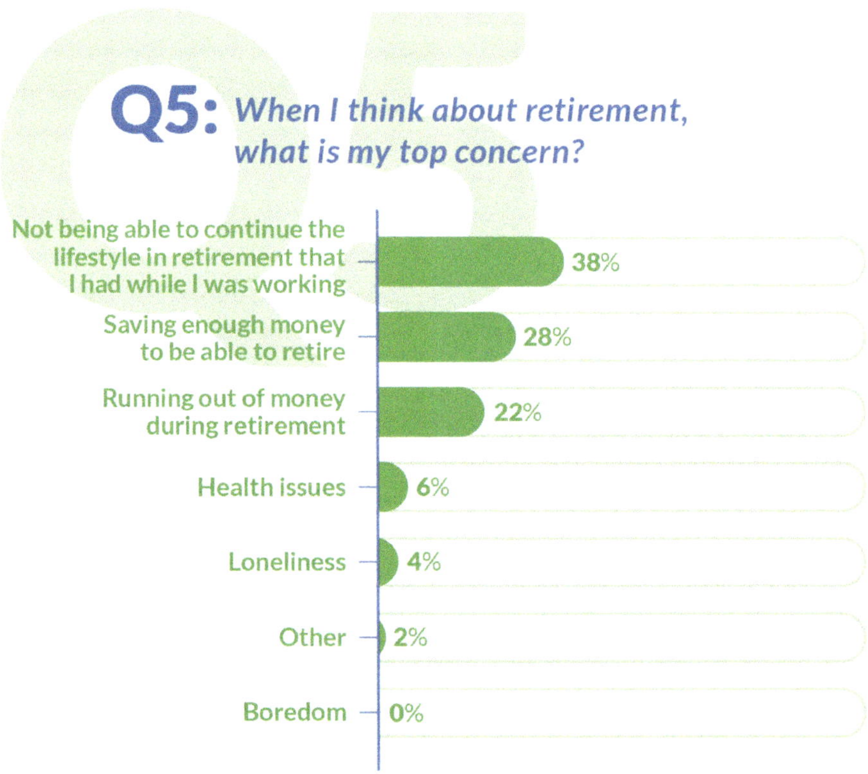

We asked this same question to our clients that are 55 or older, including clients that are retired. The top concern for our older clients was first running out of money during retirement and second was health issues. Perhaps it is not surprising that for many younger people in this survey, health issues were not yet a concern.

The exercise for this chapter is for you to list the issues you see in each of these areas and select the next steps you want to take to move forward in each area.

Real Client Story: Building a Successful Career

When you are early in your career, how should you get started building wealth?

Jeff is in the early stages of his career as a professional software marketer. He is smart, hard-working, and focused on building a successful career. At work, he manages a team and has earned the respect of his company's leadership. While he wants to succeed at his current company, he also recognizes the importance of considering other promising career opportunities that may come his way and may be even better.

Jeff's parents are our clients. They recommended that he start financial planning sooner rather than later. As a single person in his 30s, Jeff manages his spending and savings in a way that has allowed him to pay off his car loan and become completely debt-free.

Jeff's top financial goal is to plan for the future and eventually purchase his first home. That said, he realizes this may not be the ideal time given elevated home prices and high mortgage interest rates. That's why working with us has been beneficial for Jeff. He has always been good at building his personal savings and contributing to his 401(k), but he didn't know how to grow that into something more. By working with us, Jeff continues to save regularly while also investing in a diversified portfolio that matches his risk tolerance.

Jeff has advice for others starting their careers. "Make saving a normal part of your routine—even if it means starting with just a small percentage of each paycheck. I also recommend increasing your savings rate whenever you receive a raise."

Jeff is an avid traveler. He frequently visits his out-of-town family and explores interesting places outside the U.S., especially in Europe. His bucket list destinations over the next few years include Spain, Portugal, and Croatia.

Jeff is a great example of someone who makes it a priority to *Enjoy the Journey*.

Exercise:

FJP Building Wealth Framework™

Instructions: We hope the FJP Building Wealth Framework™ helps you think of steps to reach your financial goals. For each element, list issues you want to work on for your financial plan.

FJP Building Wealth Framework™	Issues	Next Steps
Values & Goals	____________	____________
Important Relationships	____________	____________
Cash Flow (Budget)	____________	____________
Goals Planning	____________	____________
Managing Investments	____________	____________
Health Insurance	____________	____________
Life Insurance	____________	____________
Education Funding	____________	____________
Estate Planning	____________	____________

4: Manage Spending to Enable Saving

Earlier in this book, we talked about saving for your goals. Making that happen requires managing your spending to leave enough money to put towards your goals in adequate amounts. Managing spending means creating a budget of how much you can spend and still have enough to save money towards all your different goals. It also means tracking your actual spending versus your planned budget to make sure your spending stays on track and is not excessive. Our experience has shown that it is difficult for some people to create a budget, track actual spending, and stay within their budget. The "B" word, for budget, is very undesirable for some people. Let's talk about this important topic in more detail.

For married couples, it is important for both to agree on how much they will spend and how they will spend their money. An excellent first step is for the couple to sit down and agree on the maximum amount that either person can spend before getting an agreement from the other person. While this may seem like a simple thing, getting agreement from both in the couple can save time in arguments later. With this completed, now is a good time to plan how your money will be spent. That means it is time to create a budget.

Creating a budget for your spending requires two things:

- creating a list of categories for your monthly spending, and
- setting a spending goal to stay below for each category.

While this can be done manually, there are excellent software programs available to make this task easier and more fun. These programs often allow you to download your actual spending transactions from your bank checking account and credit cards. These transactions can be automatically separated by category.

While there are many different programs you can use for tracking your spending, we provide our clients with a helpful software tool on our client portal. The features include automatically downloaded transactions from the person's bank checking account and credit cards. The software allows you to categorize the transactions. A monthly target for spending is set for each category. The program uses color coding to tell the user if they are ahead of target, on track, or behind target for each category.

For most people, we think it is best if they monitor and track their expenses monthly. This provides the financial discipline necessary to control spending so you can enable saving. An added advantage of monitoring your spending closely is if one of your accounts gets hacked or compromised, you can catch it quickly and stop it.

For people to save for their goals, our experience has shown that the best way to do this is to create a budget and track spending on a regular basis. We asked the people in our survey, "Do I track my spending on a regular basis?" 66% of the people said they did track their spending on a regular basis, and 34% said they did not."

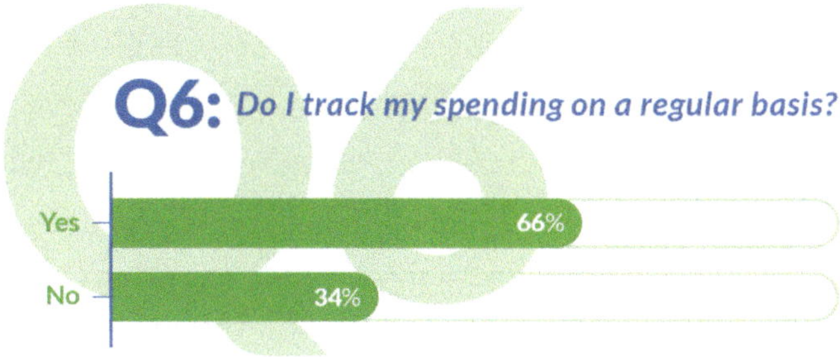

Our experience has shown that people are more successful saving towards their goals if they track and monitor their spending monthly. For the 35% of the people who are not tracking their spending regularly, we encourage them to start doing this as soon as they can.

AVOID LIVING PAYCHECK TO PAYCHECK

A surprisingly large number of people in the United States spend everything they make each month, living paycheck to paycheck. There are many problems with this choice.

1. If a person does not have an adequate emergency reserve saved, unfortunate situations such as an unplanned major car repair bill, can be a huge problem.
2. There may not be enough money left to save towards your goals, or maybe no money available to save at all.

The starting point here is to make sure that your total expenses are less than your income, with enough left over to save for an emergency reserve and save towards your goals.

We recommend having your total expenses be less than 90% of your total income, with a minimum of 10% available to save towards your goals. Getting to this point may require looking at your revenue and expenses to find a situation where you can save at least 10% of your income. If you are not in this situation, we encourage you to start by looking at your expenses, especially your discretionary expenses, to see if they can be reduced enough to start saving at least 10% of your income. You can also look at increasing your skills and finding a better-paying job or career.

SPENDING HABITS

Sometimes people ask us what is the right amount to spend. It really depends on your income. It is most important to spend less than your income. We have seen some people earn a lot of money, spend it all, and save nothing. We have seen other people with a much smaller income who spend less than their income and they are still able to save. The key point here is to spend less than you earn to have enough left over to save toward your goals.

CREATING AN EMERGENCY RESERVE

When people ask us where they should start with their savings, we recommend starting by creating an emergency reserve. Having an adequate emergency reserve can take stress out of unfortunate situations that cause a large, unplanned, and/or urgent expense. Here is a list of events that could cause you unexpected trouble.

1. Major car repair
2. A car accident requiring the replacement of the car
3. Getting laid off from your job

4. Unplanned medical expense
5. Fire in your home or apartment
6. Death of a family member

These types of situations can be very stressful when they occur. Having an emergency reserve to pay for expenses when in these situations can remove some of the stress.

The first question many people have about an emergency reserve is, "What is an appropriate amount?" We recommend an emergency reserve to cover 3 to 6 months of expenses. Your emergency reserve should be in an account that you can access immediately, with no cost to use it.

Most people have their emergency reserve in a checking or savings account at their bank. The benefit of this is that the money can be immediately moved online to their bank checking account. The interest rate on this account may be relatively low. Having access to this money quickly can be a higher priority than getting a high interest rate. The size of an emergency reserve is important. An emergency reserve that is:

- too small may be an error because it does not provide enough money during your time of need, and
- too big means that you have more money than you need sitting in a low-yield bank account when some of that money could be invested for a better return.

PAY OFF CREDIT CARDS MONTHLY

When it comes to using credit cards, the approach is simple. Only charge on your credit cards what you can pay off at the end of the month. Credit cards typically have very high interest rates. Carrying a balance past the current month means you are paying a lot of interest, and effectively paying more for an item you originally may have bought on sale. We strongly recommend paying off your credit card balance each month to avoid paying the high interest rates. This requires you to have the discipline to spend less than you earn each month. If you have an unexpectedly large expense in a month, hopefully you have enough in your emergency reserve to still pay off the credit card at the end of the month.

Many factors can influence your analysis to find the best credit card for you. Consider credit cards with low interest rates and little or no annual fee. If you travel regularly, it may make sense to get a credit card from your favorite airline, so you can accumulate miles to help pay for your flights. Some cards give you access to airline lounges, while other cards can give you discounts when booking hotels and rental cars. Some cards give you cash back on your purchases. We recommend you do research to find credit cards with benefits that are most valuable to you.

SHOULD I BUY OR LEASE A CAR?

A common question people have is "Should I buy or lease a car?" There are several important factors to consider when answering this question.

- Do you want to buy a new car, or a used car?
- Are you able to set aside money each month if a used car needs a major repair down the road?
- Are you interested in selecting the option with the lowest total cost of ownership over time?
- How long do you plan to own the car?

- Do you think the features of the car you want will significantly change over the next few years?
- What are the interest rates available for financing the car?
- How much do you have available to pay for the entire car or for a down payment?

There are three common options that people choose when buying a car.

1. Pay cash and drive the car home that day.
2. Purchase the car with a down payment and finance the rest. When you do this, the financial institution or bank that financed the loan owns the car until you pay off the loan. Comparing loan options is an important part of the process. Also take a moment to calculate how much you will have paid for the car after the loan is paid off, including interest. This will help you to budget how much to spend on the car on the front end.
3. Lease a car. For this option, the monthly payment may be lower, but you do not own the car. Rather you give the car back after the lease period, often 3 or 4 years later.

If keeping your total cost low is a priority, the important factors above are likely to lead you to the option of buying your car.

There are also factors that are non-financial that could affect your choice of car. This includes things like style, drivability, road handling, technology, and reliability. While these are all valid reasons for selecting a car, we are going to stick to the financial factors that could impact which car you select.

Total cost of ownership is the measure of all the costs related to a car. This includes the purchase price, reliability, maintenance costs, how long you can keep the car, and the cost of operating the car (gasoline for an internal combustion engine (ICE), or electricity for an electric vehicle (EV).

These are strategies to help minimize the cost of ownership for your car.

- Purchase a used car that is 2 to 5 years old and is in very good shape. When buying a car that is slightly used, you avoid the large drop in price of the car just after being purchased.
- Pay cash for the car to avoid financing charges. However, if the car loan interest rates are less than 3%, it may be worth financing the car.
- Select a model that has a history of above-average reliability to keep maintenance costs down, and be sure to ask for a vehicle history report (to see if it's been in any accidents).
- Consider an EV over an ICE car, since powering an EV car with electricity may be cheaper than powering an ICE car that uses gasoline. EV cars also have fewer moving parts than ICE cars and may have lower maintenance costs over time.
- Drive the car as long as possible, as long as it remains reliable. Some cars today can be driven over 200,000 miles with minimal costs beyond the standard recommended maintenance.

Choosing to buy a car in ways other than the above is likely to increase your total cost of ownership. Buying a car when it is new is more expensive than buying the same car that is a few years old. Buying the car with a loan has the added cost of interest on the payments, making it more expensive than buying the car with cash. However, if you can buy a car with a loan that is 0% to 2%, then that is nearly the same as paying cash and can allow you to spread out the payments of the car over time.

Leasing a car is more expensive than the plan above because you have monthly lease payments. When the term of the lease is over (after perhaps 3 or 4 years), then you must return the car and start a new lease. If you purchase a car, you can choose to keep it for 10 years or longer, after you have fully paid for the car. Some lease agreements have a maximum number of miles that can be driven each year, with payment penalties for driving additional miles that you end up owing when you return the car. So, check the details of the lease if you are interested in this option.

Knowing that leasing a car is likely more expensive than the plan above, when might it make sense to lease a car? One aspect is the certainty in knowing you shouldn't need to worry about major repairs. If technology is important to you, these features in cars change so fast that the car you want could be obsolete in a few years. Buying a car could result in a significant drop in the value of the car once the new technology arrives on the market. If you lease a car, you can turn it in to the dealer at the end of the lease and get the new car with the new technology.

If you prefer to drive a new car every 3 to 4 years, it may be more convenient for you to lease the car and turn it in at the end of the lease. Otherwise, you would need to sell or trade in the car each time you buy a new one. You may also not have a significant down payment to purchase the car. Leasing a car may allow you to get the car of your choice with a smaller amount of money up front.

PURCHASING YOUR FIRST HOME

Purchasing a first home can seem like a difficult and daunting task. Someone who is less than 30 and never owned a home told us recently, "The most pressing matter for me is how am I ever going to afford a home?" During our decades of helping people, this has historically been a very challenging financial goal. For a first-time home buyer, the price of homes can seem out of reach.

Purchasing a home in expensive states such as California can be especially difficult. We have seen some younger people who want to stay in California move to rural areas that are less expensive. We have also seen many young people move out of California, leaving family and friends behind in some cases. Moving gives them the opportunity to purchase a home in a lower-cost area. These are all part of the tradeoffs that must be considered.

The first step in buying a home is saving for the down payment. This is a very large amount of money for most young people. The thought of saving 10-20% of the cost of a home for a down payment can seem overwhelming or even impossible. If you are in this position, you are not alone. Our experience has shown that most first-time homebuyers feel very stretched when purchasing their first home. We worked for 10 years to save enough for the down payment for their first home.

There are many strategies for saving for the down payment for a first home. Some people save a set amount each month towards this goal. They understand it can take many years. Some people are in the fortunate position that they can get help with the down payment from parents or family members, or from an investment that has worked out really well. It is important to select a strategy that works for your situation.

WATCH OUT FOR SCAMS AND FRAUD

There have been so many companies that have had their customer data hacked by criminals that, for most of us, we should consider that our sensitive data has already been hacked. This means we must watch out for scams very closely. Credit cards get compromised on a regular basis. It is important to watch the transactions on all your credit cards on a regular basis. Look for spending that is not yours, but rather from criminals. Some software programs will automatically download the transactions from all your credit cards and your checking account. This allows you to monitor all these transactions in one place and avoid logging into multiple systems to look at each credit card and bank account separately.

When criminals try to take money out of your bank account, a common practice is to start with a transaction to withdraw less than a dollar. They are just testing to see if they can access your account and to see if you notice it. If nothing is done to stop them, the next withdrawal is often just under $10,000. They stay under $10,000 because financial institutions have special reporting procedures for movements of money over $10,000. Be on the lookout for these small transactions because they can be the first step by the criminals before they take a much larger amount.

REAL CLIENT STORY A Large Company Stock Position

What are the risks of a large company stock position?

Olivia and Noah are a young couple. Noah works for a technology startup company. As is the case in some of these companies, he was given shares of stock as part of his compensation package. When the company went public, the stock price shot up.

They knew that the stock price of new companies can go up or down significantly. They decided to sell some of the stock, pay the capital gains taxes from the sale, and pay off the mortgage of their home. They felt this would set them up well for the future- to have a home with no mortgage regardless of what happened in the future.

They decided to keep the remaining amount of stock. They hoped that the price would continue to grow over time. What happened is that the stock price fell by over 80%, causing the value of their stock to go from several million to a significantly lower amount. Unfortunately, the stock price of new startup companies falls more often than people think.

Olivia and Noah were very glad they had decided to sell enough stock to pay off the mortgage on their home. They regret not selling more of the stock to diversify their investments. This reminds us that a portfolio of millions in one company stock is not the same as a diversified portfolio of the same size.

We share this story to highlight the risk of having a large amount of stock in one company. We have also seen people who accumulated a lot of shares of a large technology company, and as that company grew, the value of the stock continued to grow into a significant amount of money. If the stock is in the wrong company, the stock can fall significantly and cause considerable heartache.

In the case of Olivia and Noah, they were still young, Noah was early in his career, and he had many years of working ahead of him to save for his goals. They have a home that is paid off with no mortgage, which is better than most younger couples. There was a missed opportunity for them to sell more of their company stock and create a diversified portfolio to position themselves even better for the future.

Exercise:

Creating My Budget

Instructions: This exercise is to help you create a monthly budget.

1. If you own a home, start with your mortgage costs.

Original loan amount ____________________

Year mortgage started ____________________

Years of mortgage ____________________

Mortgage completion date ____________________

Interest rate ____________________

Mortgage remaining balance ____________________

2. Now list the monthly amount of your expenses.

Monthly mortgage payment
(if owning) ____________________

Property taxes (if owning) ____________________

Rent (if renting) ____________________

Utilities ____________________

Water ____________________

Garbage ____________________

Food cost ____________________

Car payment ____________________

Gasoline ____________________

Car maintenance ____________________

Travel ____________________

Entertainment ____________________

Health insurance ____________________

Life insurance ____________________

Total Monthly Expense = ____________________

5: Saving for the Future

In Chapter 4, we discussed how to manage your spending so that after paying your living expenses, you still have money to start saving toward your goals. In this chapter, we will discuss different things for you to consider as you create a plan to save for your goals.

In our survey, we asked the question, "Do I have a set plan for saving monthly, that includes saving enough money so I can achieve my financial goals? (Using accounts such as a 401(k), Roth IRA, Bank Savings Account, etc.)

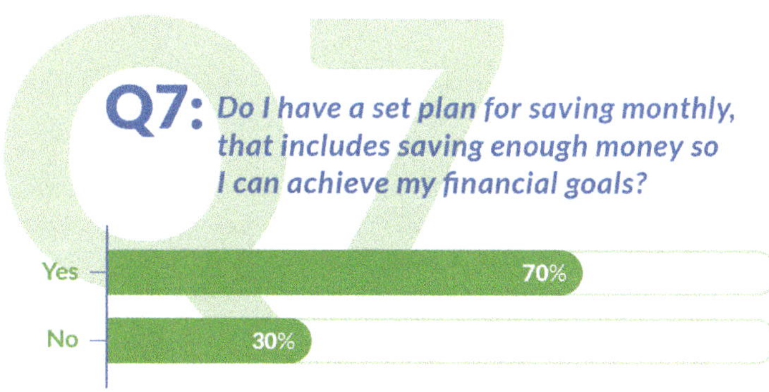

There are many ways to save for your different goals. We encourage you to start now and create a savings plan for each goal. In this chapter, we will discuss strategies for you to consider as you create your savings plan.

RULE OF 72

Let's start talking about investing with the "Rule of 72". The Rule of 72 is a simplified way to estimate how long it will take for an investment to double in value at a fixed interest rate. See the formula below.

Rule of 72 [72 ÷ *Interest Rate* = *Number of Years to Double*]

6% *doubles in* **12** *years*
8% *doubles in* **9** *years*
10% *doubles in* **7.2** *years*

As you can see, the interest rate (or rate of return) has a significant impact on how fast your money grows. While this may make a person want to become more aggressive so that their money grows faster, there have been periods in the stock market (such as 2000-2002 and 2008-2009) when the U.S. stock market lost 50%. There is a balance between risk and return. We encourage each person to invest in a way that is appropriate for them.

When it comes to saving, the starting point is to first have an adequate emergency reserve so that you can handle the unplanned expenses if unfortunate events occur. In the last chapter, we discussed how to create an emergency reserve. Once you have an adequate emergency reserve, you can start investing your money.

SELECTING APPROPRIATE INVESTMENTS

To successfully save money to achieve your goals, it is important for you to use investment strategies that are appropriate for your situation and your goals. Investments offer different levels of risk and return. It is important for you to pick investments that are appropriate for your situation and risk tolerance level.

For example, trying to save for your retirement for the long term in a money market fund that has very little return will require you to save a lot more money to reach your goal. The "Rule of 72", as stated above, says that a savings account making 2% takes 36 years to double. Growth stocks can grow at a faster rate, but typically have more risk and can lose their value at a faster rate.

One of the biggest errors we see people make is selecting investments that are not appropriate for their situation and goals. If you find that you are lacking the time, interest, and/or experience to manage your investments well, then we encourage you to get help from a financial professional. The fee you pay for a financial professional can be an excellent investment to make sure you are investing your hard-earned savings appropriately.

THE DIVERSIFICATION TRIANGLE

When selecting investments, it is important to select the appropriate investment with the appropriate amount of risk for each situation. Investments can be broken into three categories: Stability, Income and

Growth. This is called the Diversification Triangle.

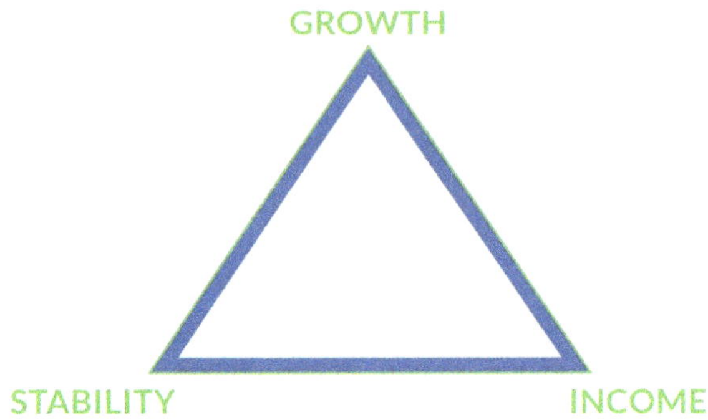

Stability investments are intended not to go down in value. They include checking accounts, savings accounts, and money market funds. They have a relatively low rate of return; however, the expectation is that they will not go down in value.

Income investments are typically some types of bonds and normally pay a dividend to provide income. A bond is like a loan that you give to a company or government. In return, they promise to pay you back later, plus interest. The investor is called a bondholder, and they lend money to a borrower. There are different types of bonds, depending on the borrower.

- Corporate Bond – the borrower is a corporation
- U.S. Treasury Bond – the borrower is the U.S. Federal Government
- Municipal Bond – the borrowers are local, city, county, and state entities

Unlike Stability investments, bonds can have periods where they go down in value. This is usually due to a change in interest rates. It can also come from the inability of the borrower to make a payment.

Growth investments are typically stocks or equity. The stock of an individual company can be purchased as one investment. A group of stocks can be purchased in a mutual fund or exchange traded fund (ETF). Both mutual funds and ETFs enable you to diversify your investments. Here is a chart that compares their features.

Feature	Mutual Fund	Exchange Traded Fund (ETF)
Structure	Group investment, priced once per day	Group investment, trades similar to a stock
Trading	Buy/sell only at the end of day	Buy/sell anytime during market hours
Fees/Expenses	Usually, higher fees and possible sales charges	Lower fees, no sales charges
Minimum Investment	May need $1,000 or more to start	Buy as little as one share
Tax Efficiency	Less tax-friendly due to selling investments inside the fund	More tax-friendly due to a special trade process
Pricing	Price set once daily after the market closes	Price changes throughout the day
Management Style	Managed by professionals selecting investments	Usually, a list of investments that tracks an index like the S&P 500

Over time, growth investments are expected to grow more than stability or income investments. They have significantly more volatility and can have periods where they drop considerably.

Developing an appropriate investment strategy requires selecting the appropriate combination of stability, income, and growth investments. Some people have the time and enjoy doing research to select the investments so they can create their own diversified investment portfolio. If you find you would prefer help in this area, we recommend you enlist the help of a financial professional. As a cautionary note, diversification strategies do not ensure a profit and may not protect against losses in a declining stock market. If you would like to learn more about investing, the Financial Industry Regulatory Authority (FINRA) offers some helpful resources at www.finra.org/investors/investing.

SAVING FOR RETIREMENT

We believe it is important to start saving for retirement as soon as you start your first full-time job. Most employers have retirement plans available. This allows you to save a portion of your income directly into your company-sponsored retirement plan. If you work for a for-profit company, the retirement plans are often 401(k) plans. If you ever wondered where this name came from, it is section 401, subsection (k) of the IRS tax code that has all the rules for these company-sponsored retirement plans. The retirement plans for workers at hospitals, nonprofits, and teachers are often covered under 403(b) plans.

Many large companies will put money into the 401(k) accounts for employees by matching some of the money the employees put into the account. This is called an employer match. The amount of the employee contribution matched may be the first 3 to 5 percent that they contribute to their account. If your employer has a company match, we highly recommend putting at least this much into your account. The company match is essentially extra money that your employer is directly adding into your retirement account. So, after you have an emergency reserve, the next place we recommend you save is in your company's retirement plan, if they provide an employee match. Contribute at least enough to get the full match from your employer. The employer match is an important part of the total compensation plan you are receiving from your company.

There are different tax rates for your income and the gains you receive when selling investments. If you take money out of most pre tax retirement plans, such as a 401(k), 403(b), or traditional IRA, the amount will be taxed as income to you. Accounts that are non-retirement accounts are typically called brokerage accounts. The taxes on the gains when you sell your investments in these accounts are known as the capital gains tax rate. Tax rates for your income tend to be higher than capital gains tax rates when selling investments. If you take money out of retirement accounts before a set age, currently 59 ½, there can also be federal and state tax penalties. You can lose as much as 50% on taxes and penalties if you take money out of retirement accounts before 59 ½. We recommend against withdrawing money from retirement accounts before age 59 ½ because of the large amount lost to taxes and penalties.

Most company 401(k) plans offer two methods for contributing to your retirement account. Money can be contributed that is pretax. This means that the money you put into your account will not be taxed as income in the year you earn it. While this is helpful to reduce your taxes in the short term, if money is taken out of your account after 59 ½, you will pay tax on all the money that comes out of this account, including your original contribution and any growth over the years.

The second method for contributing to your retirement account is after tax or Roth style. This means that the money you put into your account will be taxed in the year you earn it. While you will pay taxes on this money in the current year, the benefit is that it can grow for the long term. When money is taken out after age 59 ½, there are no taxes taken out of any money coming out of the Roth account if certain qualifications have been met. There are more nuances to the after tax contributions so if this is of interest to you, you can do more research on this or speak to your 401(k) administrator.

Money that is in an after tax account for many years, or even decades, may grow significantly. All the growth is not taxed when taken out over age 59 ½. It is difficult to know what income tax rates may be in the next few years or even decades. Having money in an after tax or Roth style account means you will not need to worry about how these tax rates will change in the future. This money will not be taxed when it comes out of the account. Because of these benefits, we are very strong supporters of saving in Roth-style accounts whenever possible.

Some smaller companies have a retirement plan that is designed for small companies, called a Simplified Employee Pension IRA, or SEP IRA. The maximum amount that can be contributed into a SEP IRA is different from a 401(k), so it is important to verify the maximum contribution limit for these plans each year. You can find the maximum contribution limits on the IRS.gov website.

If you work at a company that does not have a company retirement plan, you may be able to open your own IRA, either pre- or post-tax. Since many rules apply, we encourage you to check the most recent IRS rules for your situation. You can also get advice from a tax and/or financial professional.

If you are saving money for retirement using a retirement plan at your employer, you may also be able to save for retirement in an IRA or Roth IRA. To contribute to these plans, your income must be under the annual set limits. These income limits have increased for some years. You will need to check the income limits for the maximum income you can earn for the year before putting money into these accounts. As you can see, this part of financial planning can be very complicated. Working with a financial planner can be extremely beneficial.

START SAVING FOR RETIREMENT WHILE YOU ARE YOUNG

The best thing to do when saving for retirement is to start while you are young. This allows your investments to grow over time. Let's compare the situation for two different people, Avery and Chris, to illustrate the point.

Avery started saving at age 25. Chris started saving 10 years later. They each put the following amount in their accounts.

Age Range	Avery	Chris
25 to 35	$5,000/year	$0/year
36 to 45	$10,000/year	$10,000/year
46 to 55	$15,000/year	$15,000/year
56 to 65	$20,000/year	$20,000/year

Assume the hypothetical example of investments that each person grows at 8% per year. For simplicity, no taxes on the investments are included in this illustration.

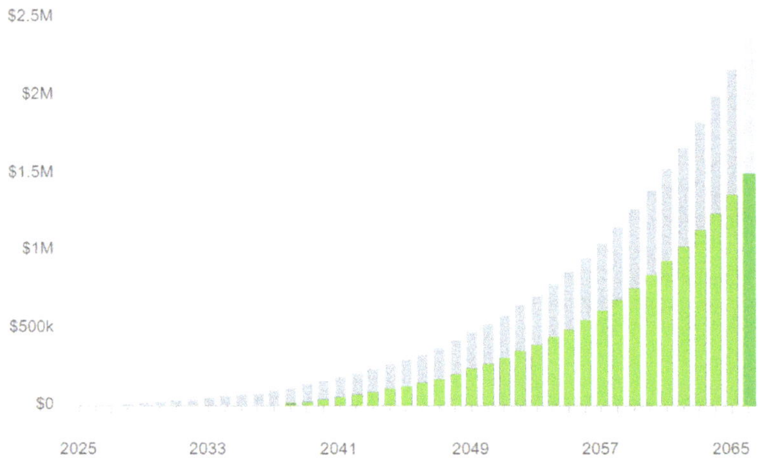

Note: Hypothetical illustration created using eMoney Advisor.

Avery's savings is shown in the light color and Chris's savings is shown in the darker color on the graph above. By age 65, Avery accumulated $2,368,747, while Chris accumulated $1,495,443. Avery invested $55,000 more than Chris between the ages of 25 and 65. However at age 65, Avery has accumulated $873,354 more for retirement. **We strongly encourage everyone to start saving for retirement as soon as they complete their schooling and begin working full-time**.

BUYING YOUR FIRST HOME

Whether you are single or married, buying your first home is likely to be a financial goal. Saving enough for a down payment may seem unattainable. Even when you have saved enough for a down payment, the monthly payment for the mortgage is usually large enough that it may stretch your budget and seem uncomfortable. We find this is normal. Most people feel this way when they buy their first home. We would like to share some suggestions that may help you if you are preparing to buy your first home.

We recommend you start the process by looking around the neighborhoods where you would like to live and getting an idea of the price. If you have kids in grades K-12 or plan to have kids in the future, research the quality of the public schools in these areas to make sure you purchase a home in a school district you like for your kids.

A mistake we have seen people make is buying a first home in an area where the home prices are more affordable; however, in this area, the public schools are below average. If you decide the local public schools are no longer acceptable when your kids are ready to attend them, it may leave you with a difficult choice. Do you move to a home in an area where the public schools are better, or pay the high cost of sending your kids to private K-12 schools? We will discuss education funding further in Chapter 7.

When buying your first home, opening a high-interest savings account for your down payment is a smart first step. Mortgage companies often want a down payment of 20%. This can seem like a large amount. To save for a down payment, it is common for people to save for 5 to 10 years. To save a down payment for your home faster, we have seen people live with their parents for a few years. This allows them to save more money by eliminating or reducing rent payments. Some people have been fortunate to get some of the money for their down payment from parents, grandparents, or other family members. Others have chosen to work at a company that rewards them with stock that has gone up significantly in value. Regardless of how you do it, we recommend you set a goal and create a specific plan to achieve it.

When you are ready to buy your home, you will most likely need to get a mortgage. Most young people start with a 30-year fixed mortgage. Spreading the payments out over 30 years may be what it takes to make the payments affordable in your budget.

A very important point that we very rarely see mentioned by financial professionals, or in books in this area, is to select a mortgage that ends roughly when you want to retire. By having your mortgage payment paid off when you retire, it will be much easier to financially afford to retire if you are not paying for a mortgage every month. When it comes to planning for retirement, we highly recommend people have a plan that lets them have their home paid off and no mortgage payments in retirement.

Let's look at a couple of examples. If you want to retire at age 65 and you are 35, getting a 30-year mortgage allows you to pay off the mortgage by the time you retire. When you are 45, let's assume you want to upgrade to a bigger home. If you still want to retire at age 65, then we recommend you get a 20-year mortgage so you can still retire at age 65. If you move to a bigger home when you are 55, and you still want to retire at age 65, then we would recommend getting a 10-year loan.

This may seem obvious and logical. Yet, we see people do the opposite. They continue to refinance their mortgage with new 30-year mortgages, so they can take out money to pay off debts. They get ready to retire at 65, and they still have 20 years or more of payments on their mortgage. This makes it very difficult to afford to retire and often results in the person having to work much longer than they wanted. While some feel it is ok to have debt when they retire, we have found most people feel much more secure retiring after they have paid off their debts.

SAVING FOR EDUCATION

If you have kids, one of your goals may be to save for their college education. There is a lot to consider in this area, and we will discuss it in more detail in Chapter 7. The important point here is that the amount you choose to save for your kid's education should be an appropriate amount when considering your other goals. For example, you would not want to save more than you need for your kid's education, while saving too little for your retirement. Please do not take on large college debt right before retirement. Your kids will have their working career to pay off their debt. You could decimate your entire retirement plans if you spend too much on your kid's college. We encourage you to complete a comprehensive financial plan so that you have the right balance of the amount to save for each of your goals.

SAVING WITH RESTRICTED STOCK OPTIONS (RSUs)

You may be fortunate to work for a larger company that offers you restricted stock options, or RSUs. An RSU is an award of stock shares, usually given as a form of employee compensation. RSUs are sometimes issued to employees through a vesting plan. This means a person needs to keep working for the company for a set amount of time for the RSU to reach its full value. RSUs that are given to employees have no value until they are vested. This is a way for the company to encourage top employees to continue working for the company. For tax purposes, the entire value of vested RSUs must be included as ordinary income in the year of vesting.

We have seen people use different strategies to build wealth using RSUs. Some people have held onto the company stock and continued to accumulate more and more stock, and work for the same company for many years. This has been a way that has successfully built large wealth for people who have worked for the large tech companies over the past 20 to 30 years. This works well when the value of the company stock grows significantly over the long term.

We have seen people accumulate company stock over many years for companies with stock that has declined significantly in value. In this case, the person lost large amounts of wealth as the company stock continued to drop. We have seen people who had millions of dollars in company stock, only to see it decline by 80% or more. Building wealth by accumulating large numbers of shares in a single stock is a very risky approach. It can work well if the company's stock grows over time. It can fail terribly if the company's stock falls over the long term. It is important to weigh the risks and rewards of this approach by evaluating the company. Consider carefully how you expect the company stock to do over the long term.

Another approach for RSUs is to sell them as soon as they become available for sale. The money can then be invested in an account with a diversified portfolio. The advantage of this approach is that it eliminates the single stock risk of having many shares of the company stock. The disadvantage may be giving up the growth potential of your company stock if it grows significantly over the long term.

REAL ESTATE INVESTMENT PROPERTY

Purchasing real estate beyond your primary residence as an investment can be a good way to diversify your investments and build wealth over time. Investing in real estate is very different from investing in stocks and bonds. Like all investments, there are pros and cons. Let's discuss a few of the basics of investing in real estate.

Here are some of the advantages of owning rental property.

Benefit	Why It Matters
Reliable income stream	Rent can create a predictable monthly cash flow. **Suggestion:** Maintain 3-6 months of property expenses in a reserve account to cover months with vacancies or major repairs.
Long-term appreciation	Real estate values historically trend upward over time, boosting net worth. **Suggestion:** Consider buying in markets with job growth, diverse industries, and supply constraints.
Tax advantages	You can deduct interest, operating expenses, depreciation, and even travel to the property. **Suggestion:** Keep meticulous records and work with a tax professional to optimize depreciation schedules.
Leverage (borrowing)	Conventional loans let you control a large asset with relatively little cash down, magnifying returns on equity when values rise. **Suggestion:** Avoid borrowing too much as it can cause problems during economic downturns.

Inflation hedge	Rents and property values often increase with inflation, helping preserve purchasing power. **Suggestion:** Include annual rent-increases (where legal) to keep pace with inflation.
Portfolio diversification	Real estate's performance may differ from stocks and bonds, smoothing out overall volatility of your assets. **Suggestion:** Avoid letting real estate property dominate your net worth.
Estate planning tool	Options for holding title of rental property, such as LLCs and revocable trusts, can facilitate generational transfers and asset protection. **Suggestion:** Coordinate with your estate plan.

Some of the disadvantages of owning rental property are the following.

Disadvantage	Risks
Illiquidity (not easily converted to cash)	Selling can take months and incur high transaction costs. **Suggestion:** Maintain ample liquidity in other parts of your investments.

Tenant and legal issues	Non-payment, eviction costs, habitability laws, and potential lawsuits are potential issues. **Suggestion:** Screen tenants thoroughly, carry landlord liability insurance, and consult an attorney on local regulations.
Maintenance & capital expenditures	Maintenance costs for roofs, HVAC, plumbing, and replacing appliances can be significant. **Suggestion:** Budget for annual repairs and schedule periodic inspections.
Market risk	Rents and prices can drop in recessions and during oversupplied markets. **Suggestion:** Diversify across locations and set conservative rent projections.
Financing risk	Rising interest rates can squeeze cash flow on adjustable loans or refinancing. **Suggestion:** Lock in fixed-rate financing and have an adequate emergency reserve.
Time commitment	Leasing, repairs, bookkeeping, and compliance can be time-consuming. **Suggestion:** Factor in a considerable amount of time or consider professional property management.
Concen-tration and disaster risk	Properties in a single market can be subject to local natural disasters or economic hardships. **Suggestion:** Consider owning rental property in different markets and carrying landlord and umbrella insurance.

If you decide to add rental property as part of your portfolio of assets, we encourage you to build a team of experienced professionals who can help you. Consider using a realtor who specializes in rental property and a professional property manager. We encourage you to do a thorough investment analysis of any property that you would consider purchasing as an investment.

We think that any real estate property purchased as an investment should have a positive cash flow (generating more income than the cost of expenses) from the very first day. A common error we see people make is limiting their options for purchasing real estate property to only their local area. Other areas of the United States beyond where you live may be a much better investment than purchasing in your local area. If you have more questions about investing in real estate, consider talking with a financial professional or realtor.

Real Client Story

Overcoming Challenges

How can I adjust my financial plan when life presents challenges?

Sabrina and her husband Linus became our clients after we worked with Sabrina's parents for many years. We always feel honored when clients ask us if we can help their adult children plan their financial future. They started their financial planning with us when they were in their 40s and they are now in their 50s.

Like their parents, Sabrina and Linus are disciplined savers. They set goals for saving and reach their targets on a regular basis. When Sabrina and Linus paid off a vehicle or something similar, they would redirect a portion of what that payment used to be to either their savings or to one of their IRAs. The ability to be disciplined savers was possible by also being disciplined spenders, and spending within their budget.

Thanks to their efforts, when we ran the numbers for their financial plan, they were on target for retirement. Sabrina and Linus told us "We are pleased with this assessment as it is one less thing to worry about. We check on our retirement accounts occasionally, but we appreciate that Scott looks out for our investments on a daily basis."

Life can present many challenges. For Sabrina and Linus, this includes kids, grandkids, and significant health issues. The benefits they have through their employers have helped them navigate through these challenges. Their employer health plans covered most of their health expenses, which were sizable. Disability benefits helped provide some income during their time off work while recovering from treatments. They are able to get very affordable life insurance through their employers.

Here is an example of Sabrina and Linus planning ahead. "Prior to any of the health issues, we had each signed up for additional health and cancer insurance during our annual enrollment period. We highly recommend this coverage as the benefits are paid to you, not to the doctors."

We have been truly impressed by their positive attitude as they worked through challenges. They and their family are committed to *Enjoy the Journey*. They recently completed two bucket list items. The first was going to a dealership and paying cash for a vehicle, and the other was a family trip to Disney World.

Exercise:

Creating My Savings Plan

Instructions: This exercise will have several steps. First, create a list of your financial goals. Next, estimate the cost of each goal. Determine how much you plan to save each month. Select the type of account or savings method for each goal.

Goal One

Goal Description: ______________________________

Cost of Goal: ______________________________

Monthly Savings: ______________________________

Type of Account: ______________________________

Goal Two

Goal Description: ______________________________

Cost of Goal: ______________________________

Monthly Savings: ______________________________

Type of Account: ______________________________

Goal Three

Goal Description: ______________________________

Cost of Goal: ______________________________

Monthly Savings: ______________________________

Type of Account: ______________________________

Goal Four

Goal Description: ______________________________

Cost of Goal: ______________________________

Monthly Savings: ______________________________

Type of Account: ______________________________

6: Insurance

There are many different types of insurance, and they are purchased for many different reasons. In general, insurance is purchased because paying a relatively small amount for the premiums can protect a person against a much larger financial hardship. Because there are so many types of insurance, people can feel like the total amount of the premiums they pay for all their insurance policies is a large amount of money.

It is very important to have the right type of insurance, providing the best of financial protection in the appropriate amount. You don't want to overpay for insurance, or pay for unnecessary insurance. At the same time, you do not want to have too little insurance in an important area or no insurance at all. Let's talk about some of the most common types of insurance so you can select the best type and amount of insurance for you.

Here are some of the most common types of insurance for you to consider.

- Health insurance
- Dental insurance
- Car insurance

- Home or renter's insurance
- Life insurance
- Umbrella insurance
- Long-term care insurance
- Travel insurance

Selecting the right type and amount of insurance is very important. Maybe there are some types on the list above that you have not considered before, or you are unfamiliar with them. While there are entire books written on these different types of insurance, we will give a brief overview of each and how you can think about them all together.

HEALTH INSURANCE

Let's start with health insurance. We think everyone should have health insurance if they can afford it. Regardless of your age, there is always the possibility of a large health expense, either from an illness or an accident. If you do not have health insurance, you could have a very large health expense that could take some or all of your assets, and leave you bankrupt.

Many people get their health insurance through their employer. For most people, this is the most economical way to get health insurance. Before you start a new job, we encourage you to understand the cost and options of health insurance offered by the company. This allows you to determine if it is adequate for your situation. If both spouses are working, many choose to keep their health insurance through their individual employers. When only one person is employed, you may be able to get health insurance for both of you through the plan from the employed spouse. If you're in this situation, it usually costs more to cover the spouse who doesn't work at the company than it does for the employee themselves.

If your company offers a variety of plans, there are a few factors that you may want to consider when selecting the plan that is the best for you.

- Is the plan a Health Maintenance Organization (HMO) or a Preferred Provider Organization (PPO)?
- If you have a preferred doctor, which plan offered by your company allows you to use this doctor?
- What is the deductible for the plan?
- Does the plan allow you to get the specific treatment or prescription drugs that are important to you?

To learn more about the health insurance plans from your company, we encourage you to talk with people at your company, such as those in Human Resources.

An HMO and PPO plan offers a network of healthcare providers you can use for your medical care. These providers have agreed to provide care for members at a certain rate. Unlike an HMO, a PPO offers you the flexibility to receive care from any provider, in or out of your network. An "in-network" doctor is a doctor who has a contract with the health insurance company to provide care at lower, pre-agreed rates. Doctors in PPO plans can be "in-network" or "out-of-network". A doctor who is "in-network" can have lower rates than an "out-of-network" doctor, within the PPO. This means you can see any doctor or specialist and use any hospital. PPOs generally do not require you to choose a primary care physician (PCP) and do not require referrals.

If you do not have health insurance offered through your employer, you may be eligible to get insurance through the Health Insurance Marketplace®. This health insurance was created by The Affordable Care Act (ACA), which was passed in 2010. You can learn more about it at HealthCare.gov.

DENTAL INSURANCE

You may have the option for dental insurance through your employer. Dental insurance covers a portion of the dental expenses if unexpected dental bills arise. These plans often have modest deductible amounts for common things such as teeth cleaning and checkups. Some employers pay for part of the dental insurance offered through their company as part of your compensation package. If this is available through your employer, we have generally found this to be affordable for most people and something you might want to consider.

CAR INSURANCE

Many different and reputable companies offer car insurance. Their prices can vary, as well as their level of coverage. We encourage you to select a reputable company that has a track record of providing excellent service, should you have partial or total damage to your car. We recommend you purchase sufficient insurance from a highly rated company. If you have a car loan, you may be required by the lender to show proof of car insurance. Most states require car insurance and a valid driver's license when owning a car.

HOME OR RENTER'S INSURANCE

A fire, hurricane, tornado, or burglary can cause significant financial expenses. These types of events can be very emotionally difficult. We have had clients or their family members experience significant loss from a fire. Each year, there are significant natural disasters around the country, including fires, hurricanes, and tornados. We recommend getting this insurance if it is affordable in your budget. Some areas of the country have higher risks of hurricanes or wildfires. This can cause home insurance to be extremely expensive. This is a difficult situation. We encourage you to evaluate all your available options to see if there is a solution that would work for you. Most home loan providers require homeowners' insurance.

LIFE INSURANCE

There is a lot to know to be able to select the amount and type of life insurance that is best for you. We encourage you to talk with a life insurance agent or licensed financial advisor **that you trust** to discuss your situation. They can assist you in evaluating the policies that might work best for you. We will cover a few basic topics related to life insurance to get you started.

There are two different types of life insurance. Term life insurance is guaranteed by the life insurance company to have a level premium that stays the same for a set number of years. These policies often last 10, 20, or 30 years. They are considered temporary life insurance policies because, for most people, they are not expected to last until the person dies.

For a Term life insurance policy, at the end of this level premium period, the policies generally have a large increase in their premium.

This can catch policyholders by surprise. As you age, the likelihood of death increases. After a 10-, 20-, or 30-year level term ends, the insurer must price the new premium based on your **current age and health risk**, not when you first bought the policy. When the level term period ends, you have several choices depending on your health, financial goals, and insurance needs.

- Continue the existing policy as an annual renewable term and pay the higher premiums.
- Buy a new term policy if you are still healthy and need the coverage.
- Convert to a permanent policy if you are in poor health and need the insurance.
- Cancel the policy if you no longer need the insurance or if it is no longer affordable.

The situation where a person might want to continue the policy could be if they were diagnosed with a terminal illness and only expect to live for a short period.

The major benefit of term life insurance is that it is the most effective type of life insurance and affordable for many people. The disadvantage is that very few term life insurance policies pay a death benefit before the level term premium period expires. Sometimes people think of term policies as renting the policy, because you pay for it for many years, and when the level term period expires, the policy owner generally cancels the policy, and there is no remaining value in the policy. To get a new term life insurance policy, most of these policies require the prospective policyholder to take a blood and urine test. Then they have to pass a process called underwriting before being offered a policy. Underwriting is the process insurance companies use to decide how risky it is to insure you and how much your policy should cost.

Some large companies offer life insurance to their employees. These are called Group Life Insurance Policies. This can sometimes be less expensive than purchasing a term life insurance policy on your own. It may also have the added benefit of not requiring the policy owner (and employee) to do a blood and urine test before getting the policy approved. The downside of company-issued life insurance is that you may not be able to continue this policy if you leave the company. We encourage you to investigate the features and benefits of these policies before you enroll.

The second type of life insurance is often called permanent insurance. This is life insurance that the policy owner intends to own for their entire life so they can collect on the death benefit when the insured person dies. These policies are much more expensive than term policies. The key point is the person is buying this for life, owning it until they die, with the full intention that when the insured person dies, the death benefit will be paid to the beneficiary of the policy after they die. Some term policies have the benefit of being able to convert to a permanent policy before they expire. We think this is a very valuable feature and if you purchase a term policy, we recommend you look for a policy with this conversion feature to give you this flexibility.

There are too many different types of permanent life insurance policies to cover here. Different life insurance companies offer many different policies with a lot of different features. We encourage you to talk with an experienced life insurance agent **that you trust**, from a reputable life insurance company. You can check the financial strength of a company by checking rating companies like AM Best and Comdex.

For some situations, it may work well to get a term life insurance policy AND a permanent life insurance policy, with an approach called stacking. For example, let's assume the person wants to get a $1 million death benefit insurance policy. Getting a $1million dollar permanent policy can be very expensive. Getting a $1 million dollar term policy may be very affordable, however at the end of the level term period, the person may have no life insurance remaining.

Let's take an example of a 30-year-old person that is married and has kids. Assume they have an insurance need of a $1 million dollar death benefit. They could choose to purchase a 30-year term policy. An advantage is that this is the most affordable way to get life insurance for the next 30 years. A disadvantage would be that it would expire with their kids while still in college.

An alternative is to purchase two life insurance policies, a smaller permanent policy and a larger term policy. In the insurance industry, they call this stacking, where one policy is added, or stacked on top of another policy. For example, you could purchase a permanent policy with a death benefit of $250,000 and a term life policy with a death benefit of $750,000. This way, when the term policy expires, you still have the remaining $250,000 permanent policy to last the rest of your life.

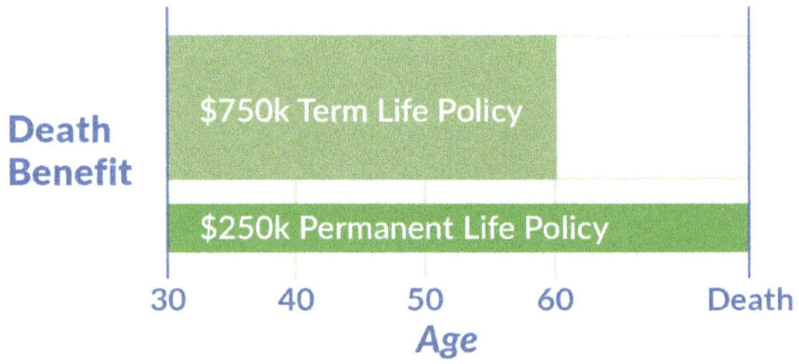

It is important to determine the proper amount of life insurance you need. We have decades of experience helping clients purchase the life insurance that is best for their situation. Having too little life insurance may result in significant hardship for your family in the event of your passing. Too much life insurance may have you spending more money on life insurance than you need and underfunding one of your other goals. Creating a comprehensive financial plan with a financial professional will allow you to calculate the right amount of life insurance that you need for your goals and specific situation.

In our survey, we asked the question, "Have I met with a life insurance agent or financial advisor to determine the best type and amount of life insurance for my situation?" In the survey, 54% of the people said yes and 46% of the people said no.

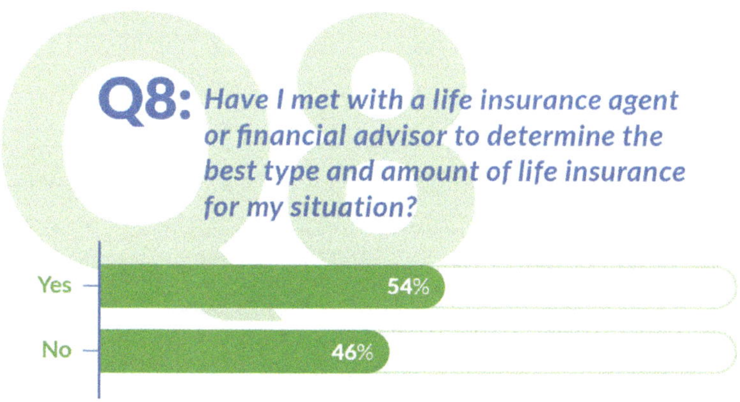

You may feel like you need life insurance. You may be unsure if you have the right amount or the right type of life insurance. We encourage you to find a life insurance agent or financial advisor **you trust** and review your situation. If you do not know one, ask your family and friends for a referral to someone they trust.

UMBRELLA INSURANCE

Umbrella insurance is extra insurance that provides protection beyond existing limits and the coverage of other insurance policies. Umbrella insurance can provide coverage for injuries, property damage, certain lawsuits, and personal liability situations. This type of insurance becomes more valuable as a person builds wealth and wants to protect their wealth from unplanned situations. Umbrella insurance can be relatively inexpensive to provide the extra layer of protection to cover your situations not covered by your other insurances. If you have an interest in this insurance, we recommend you discuss it with your insurance agent for your car or other insurances.

LONG-TERM CARE INSURANCE

Your first reaction to this may be, "I am too young for nursing home insurance". First, this insurance covers more than nursing homes. It covers care at home and in residential care facilities. Second, we recommend people buy this while they are still in their 50s, and before they turn 60. This type of insurance gets more expensive each year as you get older. It may become cost prohibitive by the time people are in their late 60s, as their health starts failing, and now they decide they want it. Also, insurance companies will only offer this to people while they are relatively healthy. If a person gets older and develops health problems, they may no longer be eligible.

If you are in your 50s, we encourage you to learn more about long-term care insurance. We find that when people are in their 50s and starting to plan for their retirement, planning for long-term care as you get older should be an important component in your retirement plan. If you want to learn more about how planning for long-term care could fit into your retirement plan, we encourage you to read our book ***Enjoy the Journey, Successful Retirement Strategies and Stories***.

TRAVEL INSURANCE

A type of insurance that has been gaining in popularity is travel insurance. This is insurance designed to protect you against the risks and financial losses that could happen while traveling. Travel insurance can protect you from unexpected costs from missed airline connections, lost baggage, medical treatment while traveling, or emergency medical evacuation.

For cruises, travel insurance can usually be purchased from the cruise line to protect you during a particular cruise. This is the same for flights. You can also purchase travel insurance from an insurance company for a particular cruise or flight. For people who travel multiple times per year, you can purchase travel insurance to cover you for all your trips for the year, and it is less expensive than buying travel insurance for each trip.

Since the COVID pandemic in 2020, we have seen many unplanned and unfortunate events occur while traveling. We recommend our clients buy travel insurance. We regularly hear stories about people who have their travel disrupted by significant weather storms or significant illnesses. For example, an illness on a cruise ship or in a foreign country can result in medical evacuation costs in the tens of thousands of dollars. Winter storms and hurricanes can leave travelers stranded for days in difficult situations. Elaine and Scott regularly purchase annual travel insurance.

We needed to use the travel insurance due to an illness just before a recent trip. Fortunately, the insurance company covered our costs in a timely manner. Some policies even cover health costs when traveling within the United States. If this type of care is important to you, then we encourage you to check the details of the benefits of the travel insurance policy. We recommend travel insurance for people who travel regularly.

REAL CLIENT STORY

Purchase Long-Term Care Insurance When Young

How can you complete two insurance needs with one policy?

Ruby and Sterling are in their mid-50s. We worked with them to create their comprehensive financial plan when they were in their early 50s. "Having long-term care insurance fits well with our overall plan. We thought we were way too late to the game since we were in our early 50s, but as we started our financial clean-up, Elaine set us up with a plan and timeline checklist of important tasks. Life insurance was on our list, and we were motivated to complete it. By getting coverage now, we've added an extra layer of protection that supports everything else we've planned for".

We explained to them that we believe an important part of planning for retirement is planning for long-term care. We recommended that they purchase long-term care insurance by their mid-50s. "We believe long-term care insurance is an essential part of our planning for retirement. It gives us peace of mind knowing that if either of us needs care later in life, we won't become a burden either financially or emotionally on each other or our three boys. We understand that the costs of long-term care can be expensive, and having insurance in place helps to protect our retirement plan. We've set out to build. Also, we currently care for our parents in their senior years and understand firsthand the responsibilities that come with long-term care. We chose a policy that has the option to use for care or have as an investment. It felt like a win-win."

We think the mid-50s is an excellent age to purchase long-term care insurance because:

- people may still be in excellent health and qualify for long-term care insurance, and
- long-term care insurance gets more expensive each year that a person waits, and it becomes much more expensive by the time a person gets to their mid-60s.

Long-term care insurance can be purchased as a stand-alone product. A stand-alone long-term care policy typically has excellent benefits that are tailored specifically to help cover the costs of long-term care. A disadvantage of this type of policy is that a person typically pays the premium for it each year. If they pass suddenly, they may not receive any benefits from the policy.

Another option is to purchase a permanent life insurance policy that will last the rest of their life. The policy owner is required to pay a premium each year for the rest of their life, and the policy will pay a death benefit when they die. There are permanent life insurance policies that also have long-term care benefits added to the policy with a rider. Such a policy can pay a death benefit if the policy holder dies, long-term care benefits if needed while they are alive, or a combination of both. A major advantage of this type of policy is that a benefit is paid one way or another, either as a death benefit or as a long-term care benefit. A disadvantage of this type of policy is that the benefits for paying for long-term care may not be quite as robust as a stand-alone long-term care policy.

Ruby and Sterling chose to purchase a life insurance policy that also has long-term care benefits. In this case, Ruby and Sterling were very healthy and qualified for a lower premium rate than expected, due to their excellent health. They also selected a policy that allows them to reduce their premium rates further by completing some activities that encourage continuing good health, such as completing an annual health checkup with their doctor. "Now that we have this life insurance with the long-term rider, we feel confident and relieved. It's one step closer to taking care of our future. We're especially appreciative that we were able to lock in a lower premium because of our good health. On top of it all, the policy rewards us for staying healthy with additional savings. We are saving money for things we were already doing. We definitely feel more in control of our future and have a feeling of peace."

"The process of getting this insurance was smooth and informative. Scott guided us through the decision. We knew nothing about life insurance, and he walked us through what we would be receiving and answered all of our questions. We also got to meet with the insurance company representative, who also answered any questions we thought of and ones we didn't. We appreciated learning all about the policy, along with the extras that would help us not only stay healthy but could also lower our premiums. Ultimately, we were able to feel confident with a policy that met our needs, qualified for great rates due to our health, and even gave us opportunities to save more by keeping up with our health. It's actually been a fun process as we continue to get to know the insurance company app and share our findings with each other."

"We aligned ourselves with the quote, The best time to start our plan was 20 years ago, the next best time is today! We thought we were too late in our planning, but were surprised to find out we were just in our right time. We strongly recommend looking into life insurance sooner rather than later. We are still in good health and able to qualify for lower premiums. Waiting too long could mean higher costs, possible health issues, or fewer options. Also, we felt it was important to work with someone who could help us understand how this type of insurance fits into our bigger financial picture. Scott and Elaine have helped us get our ducks in a row for our future. Elaine gave us a road map, and Scott guided us through the insurance steps. For us, it was about our peace of mind. We needed our children to know that we had a plan for our future selves and for them."

Exercise:

The Right Type and Amount of Insurance

Instructions: In this exercise, review the different types of insurance. For the types of insurances below, determine the features you desire for the insurance and your next step to get the insurance you need.

Type of Insurance	Features	Next Steps
Health	________________	________________
Dental	________________	________________
Car	________________	________________
Home & Renters	________________	________________
Life	________________	________________
Umbrella	________________	________________
Long-Term Care Planning	________________	________________
Travel	________________	________________

7: Education Funding

If you have kids, there are many things to consider regarding how to fund their education. There are many books written that cover the details of this topic. We want to highlight some important things for your consideration, and your plan for education funding for your kids.

Let's start by looking at funding for K-12 grades. The first question here is, "Do you want your kids to go to public schools for K-12 or private schools?" As we discussed in Chapter 5, if you purchased a home in an area with public schools that you like, public schools may provide your kids with a good education. In that case, you would not have to pay extra for them to go to a private school.

There may be a variety of reasons why you would consider sending your kids to a private school for K-12. Our advice is that if you want to send your kids to a private school for K-12, make sure you can afford it in your monthly budget. In addition to these education expenses, you want to save enough to achieve all your other financial goals, such as retirement. A mistake we have seen people make is spending a lot on K-12 education for their kids, and at the same time, saving too little for their retirement.

Consequently, they need to work much longer than they wanted to save enough to retire.

There are many different choices for your kids after high school.

- Getting a full-time job
- Going into the military
- Going to vocational schools
- Going to local city colleges or junior colleges
- Going to four-year universities

There are a lot of great opportunities to fit all the skills and goals of your kids. The most challenging financial choice here is sending kids to college, so we will focus on that next.

We see many parents and their kids start searching for a college by touring different universities. Kids can get excited about going to a particular school, only to find out the family cannot afford it. We think the best place to start is by determining what college education the family can afford. Touring schools that are beyond the financial means of the family may only lead to disappointment for the kids.

Not all parents can afford to send all their kids for four years to a major university, complete with tuition, room, and board paid for by Mom and Dad. In fact, we would say many families cannot afford this. We have seen many parents cover the full cost of a four-year college for their kids, only to end up with huge loan debt for the education of their kids. The parents sometimes do this without realizing that it crushes their retirement plan and causes significant financial problems in their later years. We have even seen parents with college loans for their kids that are so large they push the parents to the edge of bankruptcy.

With a complete, comprehensive financial and retirement plan, we hope you have an idea of what you can afford for college funding for your kids. We recommend you select a budget for the college education for your kids that does not have a large negative effect on your retirement plan. **Remember that you can get student loans for college funding, but there are no similar loans for your retirement**. If you spend too much on their college education and save too little money for your retirement, the most common way to fix this is to delay your retirement and to keep working longer than you anticipated.

Depending on the budget that you have available for college funding, there are lots of options to consider.

- Discuss with your kids the total cost of their education and how much will be paid for by the parents versus the kids.
- Decide if you can afford to send your kids for 4 years to a university.
- Apply for scholarships if your kids qualify for academic, sports or other reasons.
- Attend a local city or community college for the first two years, while living at home. They can then transfer to a major university for the final two years. Most local city colleges have very low tuition rates and are very affordable. The biggest piece to realize here is that for most careers, 4 years at a university **isn't required**. After the kids get their degree, companies may ask which university their degree is from, and not where they went to school the first two years. It is one line item on a resume filled with experience and extracurricular activities. It is perfectly acceptable for a student to start at a local community

college for two years, taking classes at **far less than the cost of a university**, and then transferring to a university for their junior and senior year. This cuts total college expenses by at least 40%.

- Participate in a co-op program available where the students alternate between working and scholastic semesters. This may extend the college period from four to five years, with the kids earn most or all the amount they need to pay for their education. Elaine and Scott were both in co-op programs to work their way through college, at the same time with different companies. We found this to be an excellent experience and recommend it to others. The student gains valuable work experience and can cover almost all of their college costs.

There are many things for your family to consider when creating the plan for your kid's college education. There are professional college counselors that can help guide families through the process of selecting a college that is best for the student and the family. Having your kid accepted at a school that makes your kid happy is a very big step for the family. It is also important that it is a college that provides them with the education and experience they want, and is affordable for the family. If this process seems overwhelming or too complex, it may make sense to talk with a financial advisor or college counselor.

Next, let's talk about ways you can save for your kid's college education. A common way to do this is by using a 529 college savings account. They are called 529 college savings plans because the rules for them are defined in section 529 of the IRS tax code. Most financial institutions offer a 529 savings plan. They are a way to save money and not pay taxes on growth when used to pay for eligible education expenses.

This can be an effective way for the kids, parents, grandparents, and friends to all contribute to saving for the education of their kids.

There are many rules for these plans. There are entire books written on this subject and how to pick a 529 plan that is best for you. If you are interested in saving for the education for your kids, we recommend you learn more about this subject to find a plan you think is best for you. Asking for help from a financial professional could also be very beneficial.

Another way to save for college education is using a non-retirement, fully taxable brokerage account that is in the name of the parents, or it is titled in the parents' Trust account. Advantages of this approach may include more investment choices, such as investing in individual growth stocks. These accounts also stay under the control of the parents and offer a high degree of flexibility. The disadvantage is that if investments are sold, the capital gains in this type of account are fully taxable, even if the funds are used to pay for college expenses. We have seen clients use both approaches successfully. If you have questions about this, we recommend you talk with a financial professional.

In our survey, we wanted to know if people had started a plan for saving for the education of their kids. We asked the question, "Have I started a plan for saving for the education of my current or future children?"

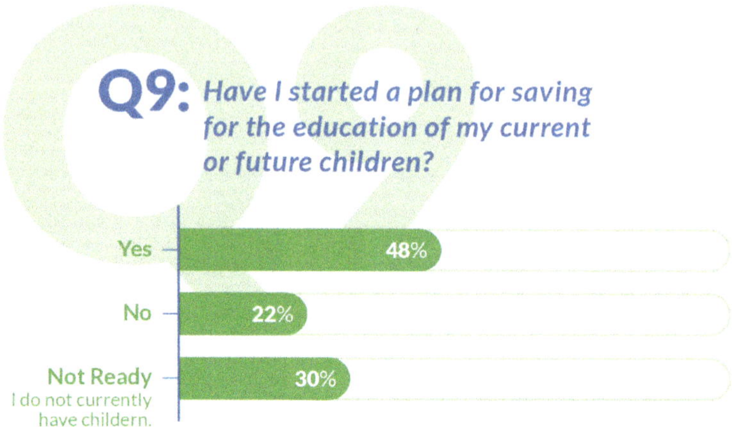

Let's summarize the key points when it comes to education funding.

- For K-12 schooling, look for a home in an area with good public schools. If you decide to send your kids to a private school, we recommend reviewing your budget to make sure the cost fits within your monthly budget and long-term financial plan.
- Determine how much you can afford to spend on college funding for your kids, and still fund your other goals, including saving for retirement.
- With your budget in mind for paying for college for your kids, select an education savings plan that fits the goals for your kids and allows your family to achieve their financial goals.

If you find that this process and making these decisions is overwhelming and you would like help, consider talking with a financial advisor and/or professional college counselor.

REAL CLIENT STORY

Save For College When the Child is Young

When is the best time to start a 529 savings plan for your new child?

When Aria and Asher had their first child, Ellie, everyone in the family was very excited, including her grandparents. The parents were very interested in starting Ellie on the right financial track, so they decided to open a 529 savings account as soon as they could.

They told us, "We wanted to be able to set up our children for success at a very early start in their lives. These days, things are very expensive, and it can take quite some time to put money away to save and accumulate. While it is in the 529, our money can continue to grow over time. There would be less time for it to do so if we contribute later in their lives, when they are closer to college age. Our main goal is to eliminate the need for them to take out educational loans and prevent them from drowning in student loan debt, a problem that plagues many people in our generation and beyond."

To open a 529 account, the child who is the beneficiary of the account must have a Social Security number. After bringing Ellie home from the hospital, they waited a few weeks until they got the new Social Security number for Ellie and immediately opened the new 529 account. Ellie's grandparents were so excited, they decided to put a sizeable amount of money in the 529 account to get it started.

A few years later, Aria and Asher had their second child, Ethan. They opened a new 529 account as soon as they could for their new son. The grandparents also added a sizeable amount to Ethan's 529 account. Now that they have a 529 account for each kid, they noted, "We feel very good about it, and wise that we have already implemented them into action for each kid. We feel we are on a good track about this, and that it will make a wonderful impact for our children down the road when it's time for them to go to college, trade school, or some other opportunity."

There are many benefits of a 529 account. There is no tax on the growth of the money when it is withdrawn from the 529 account if it is used for qualifying educational expenses. The investment company that provides the 529 account may provide a link so that anyone in the family, including all the relatives, can easily contribute to the account. It is also possible for the kid who is the beneficiary to contribute to it regularly, with extra money they get from birthdays, holidays, and/or working part-time jobs.

Aria and Asher love the feature that others can easily add to the 529 accounts for their kids. "We have let friends and family know about this and have already started mentioning it in terms of donating money at special occasions, such as birthdays or Christmas time. That way, if people don't know what kind of gift to get, they can contribute to our kids' long-term financial goals instead of guessing and getting them another toy that they may quickly set aside."

For other parents with young kids, they had this recommendation. "You can start at any time with opening a 529 for your children, but we suggest setting one up as soon as possible to allow more time and opportunities for money to grow into these 529 accounts. If you don't set them up early, you may lose time for investment and growth, miss opportunities to contribute, have other people contribute to them, and may be forced to contribute more money later to make up for the difference and reach your goals in time. If you start early, you can regularly contribute a smaller amount like $10 or $25 that shouldn't take too much away from your paycheck."

By starting a 529 savings account while a kid is young, it gives the money time to grow. Ultimately, when it is time for Ellie and Ethan to go to college, having this money available for their education may open opportunities that might not otherwise be possible.

Exercise:

College Education Funding

Instructions: In this chapter, we discussed many of the things to consider when selecting a college and planning for funding for your kid's college education. This exercise will help you determine how much the family can afford to spend to send each kid to college.

Child's Name: ______________________________

a. How many years will this kid go to college? __________

b. How much is the total cost of the college education? __________

c. How much can the parents afford to pay? __________

d. How much will the kid pay while working at school? __________

e. How much has been saved in education accounts? __________

f. How much will the family take out in student loans? __________

g. What schools and plans fit within this budget? __________

Child's Name: ______________________________

a. How many years will this kid go to college? __________

b. How much is the total cost of the college education? __________

c. How much can the parents afford to pay? __________

d. How much will the kid pay while working at school? __________

e. How much has been saved in education accounts? __________

f. How much will the family take out in student loans? __________

g. What schools and plans fit within this budget? __________

8: Estate Planning

As a reminder, an estate plan includes several documents that describe how your money and things you own (assets) will be transferred to your beneficiaries after you pass. This would include instructions so that in the event of your passing, who would receive your home and who would raise your children. With no estate plan, a judge in a Probate Court will make the important decisions for you.

Let's define some common words used in estate planning.

- **Will** - a legal document that says who should get your money, property, and belongings after you die.
- **Executor** - the person named in a Will who makes sure the person's final wishes are carried out and handles things like paying debts and distributing property after they die.
- **Living Trust** - a legal document that lets you put your assets into a Trust while you're alive, so they can be managed and passed on to others without going through the Probate Court when you die.

- **Probate Court** - a special court that determines what happens to a person's money and property after they die. It makes sure debts are paid and assets go to the right people. Whether you have a Will or don't have a Will, when you die, the process will go through the Probate Court unless you have a Living Trust.
- **Beneficiary** - the person who receives money, property, or other assets from a Will, Trust, or insurance policy when someone dies.
- **Trustee** - the person in charge of managing the money or property in a trust and making sure it's used the way the Trust says.
- **Successor Trustee** - the person who takes over managing a Trust if the original Trustee can't do it anymore, usually because of illness, death, or stepping down.
- **Power of Attorney** - a legal document that lets you give someone else the authority to make decisions for you, like handling your money or medical care. The power ends when you die. It also ends if you become incapacitated.
- **Durable Power of Attorney** - a legal document that lets someone make decisions for you—like managing your money—even if you become sick or unable to decide for yourself. This type is durable or lasting.
- **Health Care Directive** - a legal document that lets you say what kind of medical care you want if you can't speak for yourself. It allows you to name someone to make healthcare decisions for you.
- **Joint with Rights of Survivorship** - means two or more people own something together, and if one person dies, the other automatically gets their share.

Let's explain the difference between a Trustee and an Executor.

- An **Executor** carries out the instructions in a **Will** after someone dies. They handle things like paying debts, filing taxes, and giving out property to the people named in the Will. Their job ends once the estate is settled.
- A **Trustee** manages a **Trust**, which can start while someone is still alive or after they die. The Trustee takes care of the Trust's money or property and follows the instructions in the Trust, sometimes for many years.

In our experience, estate planning is the area of financial planning that is in the worst shape for most families. As a reminder, estate planning is working with an attorney to create a Will, Trust, Power of Attorney, Health Care Directive, and any other documents to make sure your heirs receive your assets in the manner you wish. Estate planning is often incomplete, out of date, or completely missing. In this chapter, we will discuss a few things to consider for your estate planning.

Most people complete their schooling and begin working without a financial focus on saving towards their financial goals. Their accumulated assets are small. They are just beginning to build their wealth. Estate planning is not a high priority. They have not yet accumulated significant assets to worry about passing anything on to someone. However, most attorneys we have spoken with recommend that a person get a basic estate plan when they turn 18, with at least a Will, Power of Attorney, and Health Care Directive. It makes it so much easier for their family to handle everything should they pass away early in life.

As a person grows older, there are a few life events that make it important to have an estate plan. The first milestone life event is having kids. If you have kids and you have no estate plan, in such a situation, there are no instructions to indicate who will raise your kid in the unlikely and unfortunate event that both parents pass at the same time. As an example, if both parents pass in a car accident or a plane crash. If such an unfortunate event occurred and you had no Will, a Probate Court judge may make significant decisions on who will be the guardians for your kids and how they will be raised. If this is concerning, we hope it motivates you to get an estate plan and then you can specify these important decisions for your kids.

Another important life event that should encourage you to get an estate plan is purchasing a home. If a single person owns a home and they do not have it titled in a Living Trust, then the home will have to pass through the Probate Court to pass on to beneficiaries. If a couple owns a home, when the first person passes, the home will belong to the surviving person. When the surviving person passes and they do not have it titled in the Living Trust, then the home will pass through the Probate Court.

When a home is sold, the owner pays a capital gains tax on the difference on the selling price and the cost basis (what they paid plus improvements). There can be a significant difference for the capital gains tax paid based on the way the house is titled and whether it is included in a Living Trust. There are many factors impacting your specific situation, including the state you live in, that can impact your capital gains tax when you sell your home. When done incorrectly, the difference can cost you hundreds of thousands of dollars. We highly recommend you discuss with an estate attorney how to title and include your home in your estate plan.

The Probate process can take 4% or more of your assets that pass through the Probate Court. The Probate Court process can also take years to complete. The attorneys we know strongly recommend that people who own a home have an estate plan with a Living Trust and that the house be titled in the name of the Trust.

When people think of an estate plan, they most commonly think of the living trust component. The Living Trust is important because it provides the directions of how you want your assets passed on to your beneficiaries in the event of your death. Another important component of an estate plan is the Health Care Directive. This provides instructions for medical professionals on how to take care of you in the event you are injured or become ill, and you are unable to make decisions about your health care on your own.

In our survey, we asked if people had an estate plan. We asked the question, "Have I completed an estate plan with an estate attorney that includes a Living Trust and Advanced Health Care Directive?"

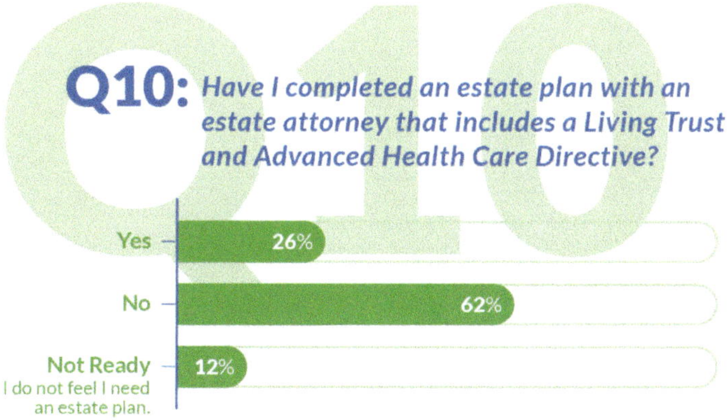

The majority of the people in the survey do not have an estate plan. To create your estate plan, we encourage you to find an estate attorney to work with you to create a plan that is specific to your situation. Different states and even different counties within a state can have different processes and procedures, so we have found it is best to work with an estate attorney within our county.

If you are not working with an estate attorney, you can ask for a referral from other family members or friends living in the county where you live. There may be benefits for different members of your family to work with the same estate attorney since they get to know your family, your situation, and the plan for your estate. If you are looking for an estate attorney, consider asking family, friends, or co-workers for a referral.

Real Client Story

Making Things Easy for My Family

How do we plan for the care of our kids if something happens unexpectedly to both parents?

When we first met Jessica and Mason, they had two young kids with no estate plan in place. We explained the importance of having one and how it helps protect their family's future. We also showed them how they could cover the cost of creating the estate plan. Since they were already gathering information for their financial plan, providing the necessary documents to the attorney was straightforward. They told us, "Our initial thoughts going in was that the process would be intimidating and overwhelming, but it was easier than anticipated. The attorney was very welcoming, walking us through each step and patiently answering the many questions we had."

For many families, the most challenging part of creating an estate plan is deciding who will care for their kids and naming a Successor Trustee. However, Jessica and Mason already had a clear support system in mind. Their delay was not due to uncertainty. Rather their life was busy, and the estate plan continually fell to the bottom of their to do list.

With their Wealth Manager, they had an honest conversation about what could happen if they both passed away unexpectedly and how the court system would take over, since they had no estate plan.

By working as a team and introducing them to a trusted estate attorney, they were able to collect the right information and finalize their estate plan within a couple of weeks.

Now, they have peace of mind knowing everything is in order, clearly documented, and that things will go much more smoothly if the unexpected happens. Jessica and Mason said, "Having an estate plan in place has given us peace of mind that our kids will be well taken care of if the unthinkable happens. The reassurance has led to an increase in date nights and short getaways, which has been healthy for our relationship."

Jessica and Mason have these words of wisdom for other young couples. "Life is unpredictable, and there's rarely a 'perfect' time to tackle an estate plan. Having a plan in place protects your loved ones and isn't just about money; it's about making sure your children are cared for and your wishes are honored. It's easier than you think and brings real peace of mind. We're very proud to have tackled this milestone. It can be an uncomfortable conversation for many, especially at our age, but it's something we felt was important."

Exercise:

Estate Planning

Instructions: We recommend you work with an estate attorney when you are ready to create your estate plan. Here are a few things to consider and prepare before you meet with the estate attorney.

Steps for Preparing for a Meeting with Your Estate Attorney

Who would be the best person to select as the Executor to be responsible for settling my estate in the event of my death?

____

____

____

If I have kids, who would I want to raise them if both parents were to pass at the same time?

____

____

____

If I own a home, what should happen to the home if both parents were to pass at the same time?

If I were to become critically ill, what instructions would I want to leave in my health care directive for my care?

Create a list or spreadsheet of assets to list in my estate plan. Include account numbers, web links, contact persons, etc., for financial accounts.

9: Creating a Plan for Success

Now it is time for you to create a comprehensive retirement plan. This plan should be designed to give you the best chance to achieve your goals. It will also address the concerns and problems that could keep you from reaching your goals. We said this earlier in the book, and we are saying it again to add emphasis. **We believe planning gives you the greatest chance for success so you can reach your goals and Enjoy the Journey along the way**.

We have created The Building Wealth Framework™ to walk you through the important and essential steps in creating your financial plan that will allow you to build your wealth.

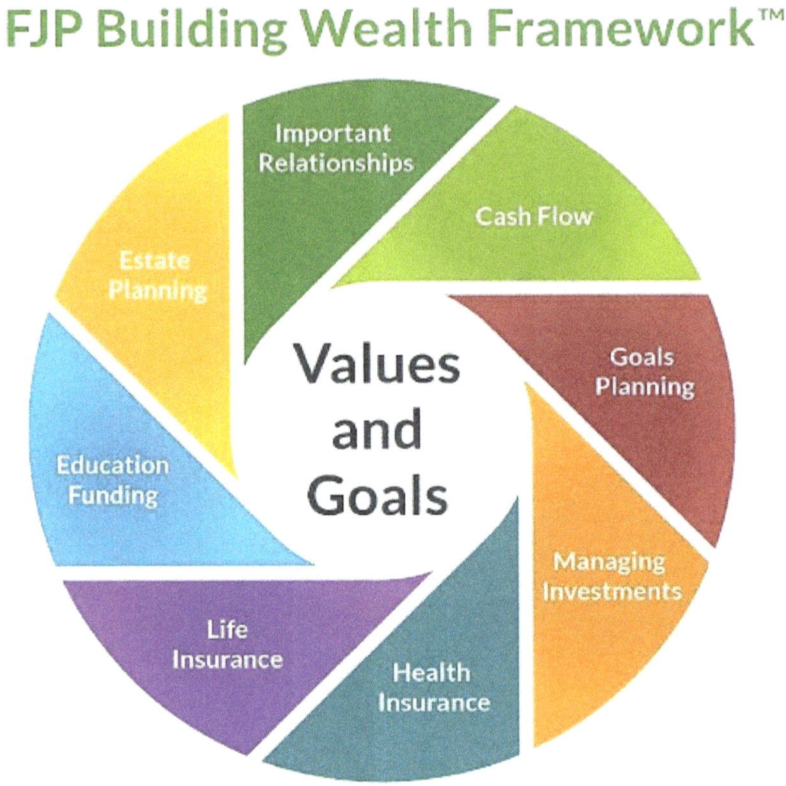

In the earlier chapters of this book, we have discussed the elements we believe are important for creating a successful financial plan to reach your goals. To summarize them again here, we recommend you start with your values and goals. To get clear on your values, we have the exercise in Chapter 1, "What do I want my money to do for me? You can define your goals with the exercise in Chapter 2, "What are my goals? Now think bigger!" If you have not completed these exercises, we recommend you do them now.

After you are clear on your values and goals, we recommend working on these essential elements for your plan.

- Important relationships
- Cash flow
- Goals planning
- Managing investments
- Health insurance
- Life insurance
- Education funding
- Estate planning

We believe the best financial plans are comprehensive and include all these areas. For people who have come to meet with us, a common error is that they are missing one or more of these essential elements listed above. It is critically important that your financial planning includes all these elements. Any missing elements can create significant problems.

While your plan can have all these elements, it is important that each element is optimized so that it fits correctly within the overall plan. For example, saving too much for one goal and saving too little for another goal may create unintended problems down the road. When you are young and entering your working career, your situation may be relatively simple. You may find that identifying your goals and saving as much as you can is a good financial plan.

As you grow older and build wealth, your situation is likely to grow more complex. There will come a time when it makes sense to do more comprehensive financial planning. This is often the time when people decide to work with a financial professional. They can help you run the numbers and look at scenarios to create a comprehensive financial plan that is tailored to your specific situation. Waiting until later in life can result in missed opportunities and making wrong financial decisions.

We asked the people in our survey if they have completed a comprehensive financial plan. We asked the question, "Have I completed a comprehensive plan to prepare me to reach my financial goals and for retirement?"

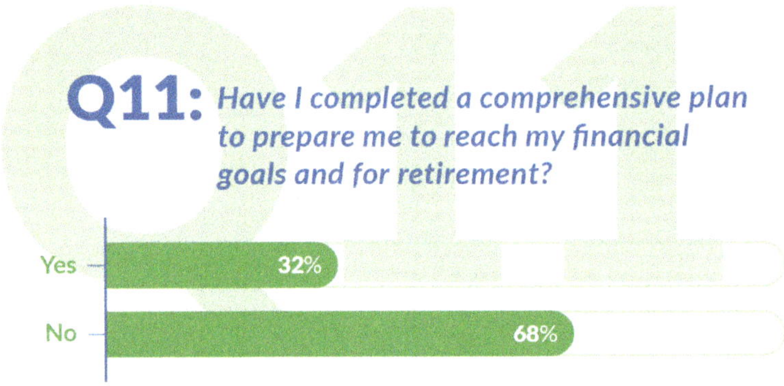

As might be expected in the survey, the percentage of people that have completed a comprehensive financial plan increased for the older age groups.

Have a plan?	25-35	36-45	46-55
Yes	10%	35%	47%
No	90%	65%	53%

We think the numbers above show that there is an opportunity for people to do financial planning earlier in life to help them reach their goals.

As you progress through your working career, there are some important things to consider completing before retirement. We asked the people in the survey, "What do I feel is important to complete prior to my retirement? (Select all that apply)." Here are the results.

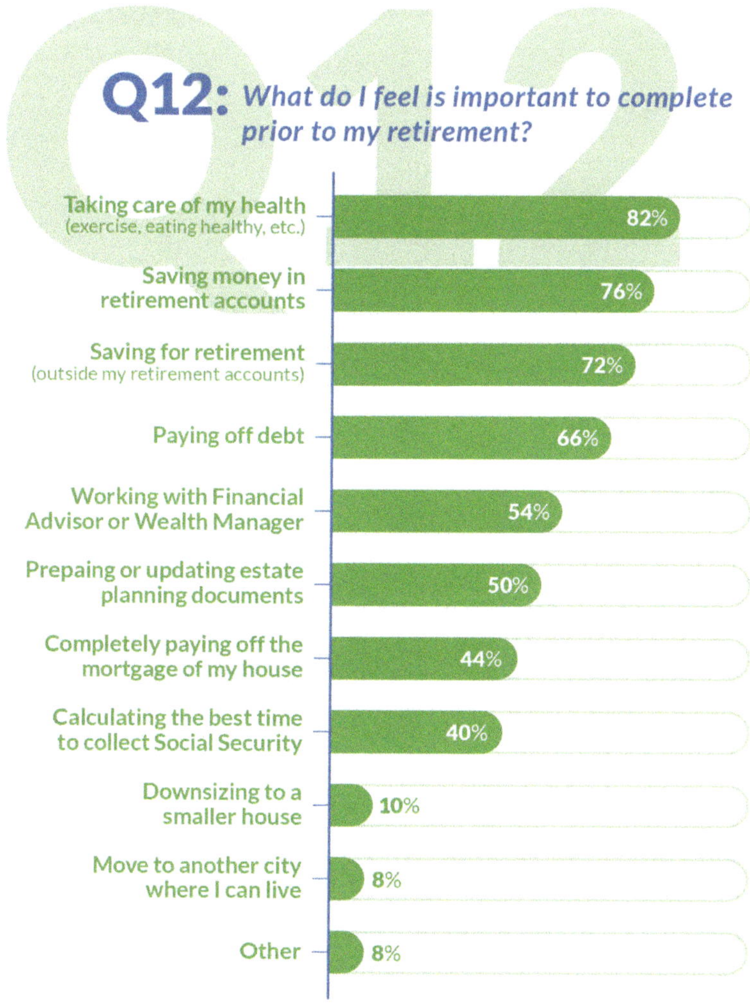

This provides a list for you to consider as you create your plan for retirement.

Have you considered how you want to spend your time in retirement? What are your goals during your retirement? We asked the people in the survey, "What am I looking forward to most during my retirement? (Rank from most important to least important)."

Perhaps this list will provide you with some things to consider as you create goals for the retirement phase of your life.

From our experience, we have found it is important for you to build a team of professionals to help you. We recommend you consider including the following professionals.

- Financial professional
- Estate attorney
- Tax professional (Enrolled Agent or CPA)
- Insurance agents (Home, health, auto, life, long-term care)
- Primary health care provider
- College counselor

As you build wealth and your situation becomes more complex, we encourage you to build a team of professionals to help you reach your goals.

If you want to begin working on your financial plan, we have created exercises for each chapter in this book. To make it easier for you to complete the exercises, you can download a complimentary workbook. You can use this workbook to complete the exercises in this book at the website www.financialjourney.com/books.

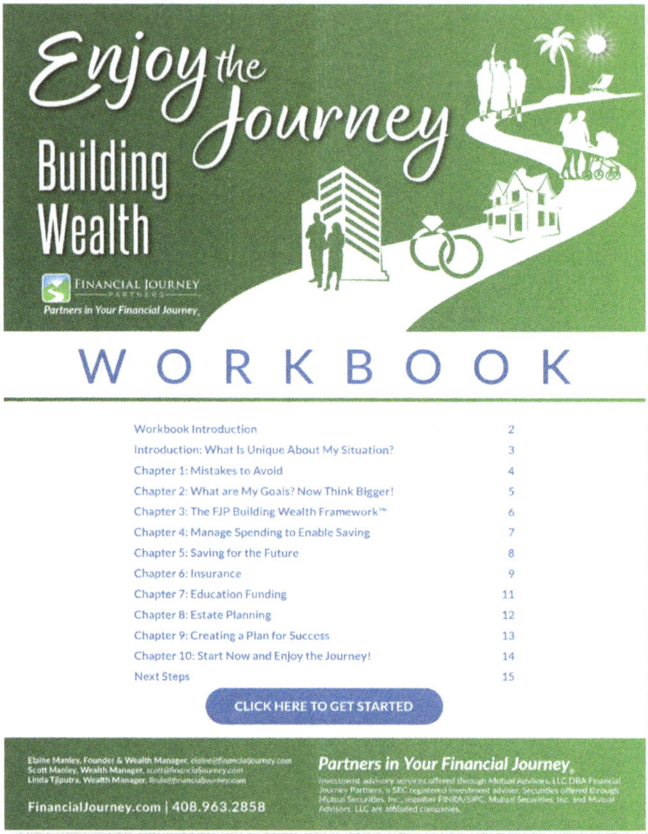

Enjoy the Journey

Building Wealth

FINANCIAL JOURNEY PARTNERS

Partners in Your Financial Journey

WORKBOOK

CLICK HERE TO GET STARTED

Elaine Manley, Founder & Wealth Manager, elaine@financialjourney.com
Scott Manley, Wealth Manager, scott@financialjourney.com
Linda Tjiputra, Wealth Manager, linda@financialjourney.com

FinancialJourney.com | 408.963.2858

Partners in Your Financial Journey®

Investment advisory services offered through Mutual Advisors, LLC DBA Financial Journey Partners, a SEC registered investment adviser. Securities offered through Mutual Securities, Inc., member FINRA/SIPC. Mutual Securities, Inc. and Mutual Advisors, LLC are affiliated companies.

We have written additional books that may help you. When a person retires within 5 years, now the focus shifts to making the transition from the working part of life to the next phase of life. That may be retirement, starting a second career or some other major change. To help a person plan and implement this major change, we wrote the book ***Enjoy the Journey, Successful Retirement Strategies and Stories***.

This book provides a framework with the important elements to successfully make this transition. It includes real client stories of people who have made the successful transition to retirement. It also includes exercises to help think through the important decisions when making this transition. This book is available on Amazon in eBook, paperback, and hard copy.

You can download a complimentary workbook to use when completing the exercises in the book at the website www.financialjourney.com/books.

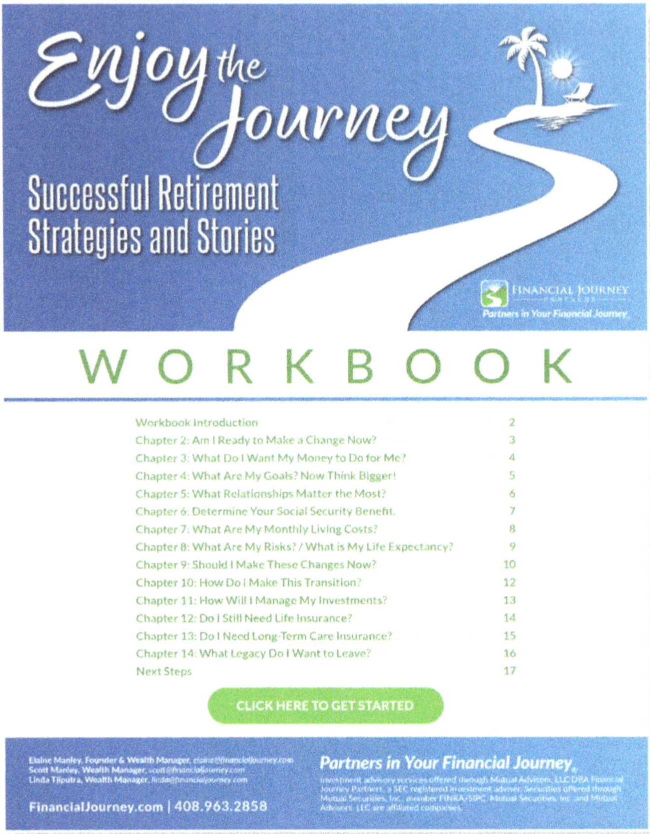
Enjoy the Journey

Successful Retirement Strategies and Stories

FINANCIAL JOURNEY PARTNERS

Partners in Your Financial Journey

WORKBOOK

CLICK HERE TO GET STARTED

Elaine Manley, Founder & Wealth Manager, elaine@financialjourney.com
Scott Manley, Wealth Manager, scott@financialjourney.com
Linda Tjiputra, Wealth Manager, linda@financialjourney.com

FinancialJourney.com | 408.963.2858

Partners in Your Financial Journey®

Investment advisory services offered through Mutual Advisors, LLC DBA Financial Journey Partners, a SEC registered investment adviser. Securities offered through Mutual Securities, Inc., member FINRA/SIPC. Mutual Securities, Inc. and Mutual Advisors, LLC are affiliated companies.

This workbook is a PDF that you can download and type in your answers as you complete the exercises in this book.

We have been helping women successfully plan and implement their retirement strategies for decades. What our experience has taught us is that when it is time to plan and take the big step to retirement, there are some things that are unique to women. The experience of our women wealth managers has made us keenly aware of this. We use our years of experience to help women avoid the pitfalls and implement the retirement of their dreams.

To do this, we wrote the book ***Enjoy the Journey, A Woman's Guide to Retirement***. Many women view money differently than men. In our many years working with women, we have found that women experience more feelings, emotions and compassion when discussing their retirement. It's not just about the numbers. Retirement is literally a way of life.

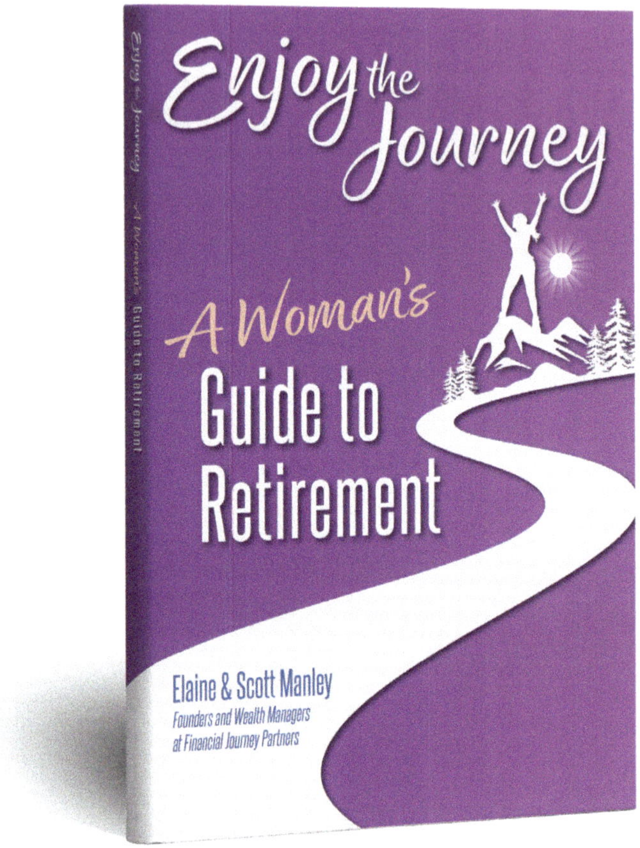

You can also download a complimentary workbook to use when completing the exercises in this book at the website www.financialjourney.com/books.

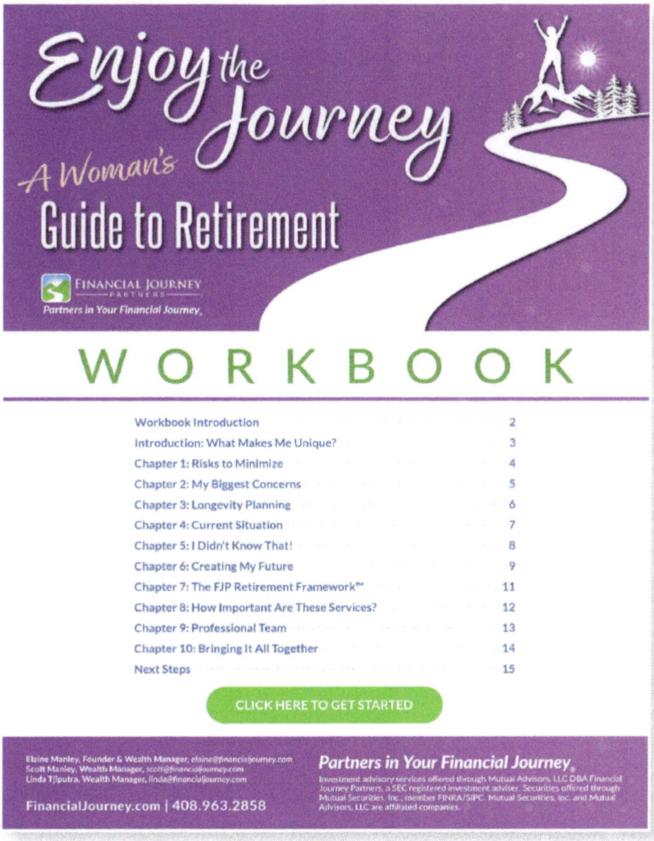

This workbook is also a PDF that you can download and type in your answers as you complete the exercises in this book.

For our women clients, we are their financial professionals. Our role is to help our clients make smart decisions and align their money with their goals so they can *Enjoy the Journey*. We want to help our clients do the things that are most important to them and help them achieve their goals faster than they thought was possible.

REAL CLIENT STORY

Start Financial Planning When You are Young

What things should a young couple consider when creating their financial plan?

Rachel and Ross started their financial planning at a very young age. They were renting, did not yet have kids, and they wanted to buy a house. They started saving immediately. They tracked all their spending with a spreadsheet so they could see how much they were spending. "It helped us be fiscally responsible and mindful of our spending," said Ross.

They began working with Linda Tjiputra, a Wealth Manager at Financial Journey Partners, at a young age to create their financial plan. "We have been taking a more structured, formal approach since working with Linda," said Ross. Rachel added, "Linda has really helped us make sure we have all these things in place."

Rachel and Ross now have two kids. They worked with their Wealth Manager, Linda, and they accomplished many goals in their financial plan.

- Buying a first home
- Upgrading to a larger home
- Refinancing student loans

- Saving the maximum into their 401 (k) retirement accounts at work
- Understanding how their RSUs work from their company
- Setting up 529 college savings accounts for their kids
- Getting life insurance for both parents and both kids
- Using a tax professional since their financial situation has grown beyond using TurboTax
- Getting an Estate Plan to protect their family, kids and assets
- Investing in rental property with a family member

Their financial plan shows that they are on track for their retirement, and they are still in their early 40s. From our experience, it is rare for people of this age to have so many elements of their financial plan in place. Even more important, their financial plan shows they are on track for the retirement of their dreams.

When we asked them what financial accomplishments they are most proud of, they said the following.

Rachel – "Owning a home, having a stable home for the kids and having 529 plans for their college education. I feel we are set up well for anything that comes our way now or in the future. We both have jobs at tech companies and there is so much change in the market right now that we are well equipped to handle any ups or downs that come our way."

Ross – "I feel much less stressed about things. We have done things the right way and I know we are on the right path. I know that our kids are taken care of if something happens to us."

The next goal that Rachel and Ross are working on is retirement. Ross noted "The main goal is retirement. Ideally, we would like to retire as soon as possible, but we want to make sure we have our children's needs covered first." Rachel added, "We are working on early retirement! Long term I'd love to be able to work less (part-time or being a stay-at-home parent) so I can spend more time with the kids."

We asked Rachel and Ross what advice they have for other young couples who are working on their financial plan. Ross said, "My biggest piece of advice would be to understand what options you have for saving, be aware of where your money is going, and to trust the process. It can feel overwhelming at times, but if you take one step at a time and do whatever you can as early as you can and commit to your plan, then your financial stability will increase over time. I believe in the adage 'do what you have to do now so that you can do what you want to do later.' This means putting in the time and effort now so that you can set yourself up for success later in life." Rachel added, "What Ross said! But also, start small - focus on one thing at a time and work your way from there. Is it creating a plan for savings? Setting up life insurance? Trying to do it all at once can be overwhelming."

Rachel and Ross noticed that other young couples they talk with often do not know about all these things because they do not have a Wealth Manager like Linda guiding them along the way. A great place to start is reading this book and completing the exercises at the end of each chapter. We love to see young couples starting their financial journey the right way!

Exercise:

Summarizing the Key Elements

Instructions: There are many components in a comprehensive financial plan. To get started, here are a few important questions for you to answer. Now that you have read this book, it is time to put your plans in place and act. Whether you are just starting your career or closer to the end, let's recap some of the most important things to consider in your next steps.

What are my top financial goals?

____

At what age would I like to retire?

____

Based on where I am financially today, at what age do I think I will be able to retire?

____

When I think about my retirement, what is my top concern?

____

Do I track my spending on a regular basis?

____

How much should I save towards each goal?

Do I have the right amount and type of life insurance?

Do I need an estate plan or update an existing plan?

10: Start Now and Enjoy the Journey!

This book was written for people aged 25 to 55 to help you build wealth. You may be near the start of your career, or you may be closer to the end. In either case, we encourage you to start planning NOW! Time goes by faster than you think. You may be able to do this planning on your own, or you may find that you want help. Either way, the important thing is to get started.

We created the FJP Building Wealth Framework™ based on our decades of experience. It includes the essential elements to consider when you create your financial plan. Think about what is important to you, set your goals, and identify the people who are important to you. The exercises in this book were designed to guide you through the important questions to think about as you plan to build wealth.

We hope that your excitement grows as you set big goals and make tangible plans to achieve them. **The exercises in this book were designed to help you achieve your goals and accomplish more than you ever**

thought possible. You may reach a point where you need help with your financial planning. You may be asking yourself, "Should I use a Wealth Manager to help me create and implement my plan?" If you decide you want to work with a Wealth Manager, here are things to consider when selecting someone.

We recommend you work with a Wealth Manager who is a fiduciary. A Wealth Manager who is a fiduciary is required by the financial regulators to put their client's interests first. A fiduciary is independent and does not work for a company that requires them to sell the products of that company. For example, financial advisors who work for insurance companies or divisions of a bank that sell proprietary products from their company are not fiduciaries. At Financial Journey Partners, we are not employees of a firm that sell proprietary products. That allows us to select the products we feel are the most appropriate for our clients and put the interests of our clients first.

There are also many different types of financial professionals. Brokers may only help their clients buy and sell stocks and bonds. Some financial advisors may provide a limited level of financial planning for their clients.

At Financial Journey Partners, our financial professionals are Wealth Managers. We offer active management of a wide range of investments, from many of the largest financial companies. We provide advanced, comprehensive financial planning using sophisticated financial planning software.

What sets us apart in our industry is that we also work with a network of professionals with whom we partner to help our clients:

- mitigate taxes,
- efficiently transfer wealth through estate planning,
- protect wealth from being taken away unjustly, and
- maximize your charitable impact.

We spend a significant amount of time vetting professionals who provide the services needed by our clients. This includes professionals for estate planning, tax preparation, travel agents, and more. We collaborate with these professionals, so our clients feel they have a team of professionals that are working together to help them.

In addition to expecting competent and experienced professionals, our women clients care about the personality of their financial professional. Our clients are sensitive to how they are treated. They are appreciative of the extra time we spend identifying other professionals to round out their team. These are professionals that have more empathy and can explain things well, without "talking down" to them.

We completely understand that this is about so much more than money for you and your family. We will challenge and support you to think about bigger possibilities that are aligned with who you are. Our goal is to help our clients make smart financial decisions and help them implement those decisions as smoothly as possible. Our team provides an exceptional level of service for our clients. At Financial Journey Partners, we work with a select group of families that are looking for a long-term relationship with a Wealth Manager. For our clients, we want to be *Partners in Your Financial Journey®*.

We host educational and fun events throughout the year to build a sense of community for our clients. It is an opportunity for clients to talk with other families that may be in similar situations. Since many clients refer their friends and family members, our client events provide opportunities for our other clients to get together with their family and friends, who are also clients. We even have an FJP Women's Group to encourage that sense of community among our women clients. They find enjoyable activities to do together, like Pickleball, hiking in our beautiful area, and more.

We have been working with clients for decades. We are known for helping our clients make smart decisions so they can align their money with their goals and *Enjoy the Journey* along the way. Smart decisions are based on a deeper understanding of who and what are important to you. It enables us to help guide you, whether through conversations or scenario planning, to help you make the best choices. What we mean by *Enjoy the Journey* is making sure you do the things you've been wanting to do, and possibly sooner rather than later. We want our clients to *Enjoy the Journey* throughout their lives, doing the things that are important to them.

If you're ready to start now to plan your financial future, you can schedule a complimentary introductory meeting with us on our website at www.financialjourney.com or call us at 408-963-2858. If we can help you, we'll let you know, and if we are not the right fit, we will do our best to introduce you to someone who might be a better fit to help you.

You are young and your life is full of opportunities and possibilities. We want you to live the life of your dreams. We want you to achieve your goals and accomplish more than you ever considered possible. Think big! Dream big! Then create a plan to achieve it all. And remember, along the way, we encourage you to *Enjoy the Journey!*

To your future!
Elaine and Scott Manley

Exercise:

Bringing it All Together

Instructions: Now is the time to put your plans in place and act. Whether you are just starting your career or closer to the end, now is the time to create a plan. Document your next steps and list any professionals you need to help you in each area.

FJP Building Wealth Framework™	Next Steps	Professional
Values & Goals	______________	______________
Important Relationships	______________	______________
Cash Flow (Budget)	______________	______________
Goals Planning	______________	______________
Managing Investments	______________	______________
Health Insurance	______________	______________
Life Insurance	______________	______________
Education Funding	______________	______________
Estate Planning	______________	______________

Appendix 1

In late 2025, we surveyed 50 people ages 25 to 55 to get their views related to financial issues and retirement. The analysis of the survey results is spread throughout the chapters of this book. This is a summary of the answers to each question.

1. What is my biggest concern about building wealth before my retirement?

   By far, the most common answer was some variation of not having enough money to meet their goals. Here are examples.

   - not having enough money for retirement
   - not having enough money to live comfortably when retired
   - having investments long enough
   - having enough money with the increasingly high cost of living

2. What are my top financial goals? (Rank in order of importance)

   7.9 – Creating an adequate emergency reserve for the unexpected
   7.7 – Saving for retirement
   6.1 – Paying off student loans
   6.0 – Saving for the college education of my current or future children
   5.8 – Buying a house or condo
   5.8 – Having one or more children
   5.2 – Taking care of parents
   4.5 – Buying a car
   4.3 – Paying for a wedding ring and wedding

3. At what age would I like to retire?

   The age people would like to retire ranged from 50 to 75. The average age was 61.

4. Based on where I am financially today, at what age do I think I will be able to retire?

   The age people think they will financially be able to retire ranged from 50 to never. The average age was 66.

5. When I think about my retirement, what is my top concern? (Select One)

   38% – Not being able to continue the lifestyle in retirement that I had while I was working

   28% – Saving enough to be able to retire

   22% – Running out of money during retirement

   6% – Health issues

   4% – Loneliness

   2% – Other

   0% – Boredom

6. Do I track my spending on a regular basis?

   66% – Yes

   34% – No

7. Do I have a set plan for saving monthly that includes saving enough money so that I can achieve my financial goals? (Using accounts such as a 401(k), Roth IRA, Bank Savings Account, etc.)

   70% – Yes

   30% – No

8. Have I met with a life insurance agent or financial advisor to determine the best type and amount of life insurance for my situation?

   54% – Yes

   46% – No

9. Have I started a plan for saving for the education of my current or future children?

   48% – Yes, I have a savings plan for each of my children

   22% – No, I do not have a college savings plan for each of my children

   30% – I do not currently have children, so I am not ready to start saving for college

10. Have I completed an estate plan with an estate attorney that includes a living trust and an advanced health care directive?

   26% – Yes

   62% – No

   12% – I don't feel I need an estate plan

11. Have I completed a comprehensive financial plan to prepare me to reach my financial goals and for retirement?

   32% – Yes

   68% – No

12. What do I feel is important to complete prior to my retirement? (Select all that apply.)

   82% – Take care of my health (exercising, eating healthy, etc.)

   76% – Saving money in my retirement accounts

   72% – Saving for retirement (outside my retirement accounts)

   66% – Pay off debt

54% – Work with a Financial Advisor or Wealth Manager

50% – Preparing or updating estate planning documents

44% – Completely paying off the mortgage of my house

40% – Calculate the best time to collect Social Security

10% – Downsize to a smaller house

8% – Where I can live

8% – Other

13. What am I looking forward to most during my retirement? (Rank from most important to least important)

    9.6 – Spending time with family and friends

    8.8 – Travel

    7.3 – Having more free time

    7.3 – Having less stress

    6.7 – Relaxing

    6.4 – Pursuing new hobbies

    6.4 – Romance and dating

    5.8 – Volunteering

    5.4 – Hiking and being outdoors

    4.4 – Playing sports

    3.1 – Watching more TV, movies, and sporting events

14. Am I currently a client of Financial Journey Partners?

    24% – Yes

    76% – No

15. What is my age?

    10 – 25 to 35

    23 – 36 to 45

    16 – 46 to 55

16. Am I currently married?

    66% – Yes

    34% – No

17. Do I currently have children?

    66% – Yes

    34% – No

18. Do I own a house or condo?

    62% – Yes

    38% – No

Special Thanks

We are grateful to all the people who have helped us with the creation of this book. Special thanks to Scott's sister, Paula Manley, who helped us with multiple rounds of editing this book and provided many helpful suggestions.

We also thank Linda Tjiputra, a Wealth Manager at Financial Journey, for her caring, compassion, and expertise when working with her clients. Her passion for helping her clients shines through in the "Real Client Stories" from her clients that are in this book.

Other people we would like to thank are John Bowen and Jon Powell, and the team at CEG. This group is dedicated to helping Wealth Managers create a fantastic experience for their clients. They also help us improve our business processes. We are grateful for all their help and support over the years.

Thank you, Nick Fryer, for the beautiful graphics on the cover and inside the book. Thank you, Mario Fachini, for guiding us on the development and distribution of our book.

We really appreciate our clients who have allowed us to tell their stories of how they have worked hard, planned well, and are on track while also enjoying the game of life. We also want to thank the amazing team at Financial Journey Partners who work very hard every day to give our clients a great experience.

About the Authors

Elaine Manley

Elaine is the founder and the senior Wealth Manager at Financial Journey Partners. She paid for her college education by working in a co-op program at General Motors Institute, where she got her bachelor's degree in finance and industrial administration. She started her career in the Accounting Department at a General Motors division in the Midwest. One day with the wind chill hitting 35 below zero, Elaine decided to move to warmer weather. Having been to Silicon Valley a year earlier and loving the area, she chose to move to Sunnyvale, CA and began working in the Accounting Department at Hewlett-Packard.

Elaine decided quickly that her passion was not to work for a large corporation. She found it much more important to help improve people's lives and help them achieve their goals and dreams. She started her career in 1986 as a financial advisor at a national financial firm. Over the years, she grew her practice to be one of the largest in the firm.

In 2018, Elaine started her own firm, Financial Journey Partners. This name was selected because the goal of the firm is to develop long-term relationships with clients and be their partner on their financial journey. Starting her own firm allowed her to use her decades of experience to design a firm around the needs of her clients, including building an office that is unlike others in the industry and provides a friendly atmosphere that makes clients feel at home.

In 2022, the Silicon Valley Business Journal selected Elaine as one of their 2022 Women of Influence. The women selected are leaders of companies and institutions from their different industries in Silicon Valley. Elaine was the only Wealth Manager selected in the group in 2022. This award recognizes women who are established business leaders with a strong record of innovation in their fields, outstanding business performance, and a clear track record of meaningful community involvement. These women have made a difference in their communities, blazed a trail for other women, and are making a positive impact in Silicon Valley. She is honored to be among this group of women.

Scott Manley

Scott joined Elaine as a financial advisor in 2000. He attended the University of Wisconsin in Madison. Like Elaine, he also worked in a co-op program to pay for his education. After getting a bachelor's degree in mechanical engineering, he continued his studies to get a master's degree in business administration.

Looking to leave the cold Wisconsin winters (similar to Elaine), Scott accepted an engineering position at Hewlett-Packard. As luck would have it, Elaine and Scott worked at the same site at HP. Their lives were on a parallel track, and it led them both to HP. They met, fell in love, and the rest is history.

Scott was able to see firsthand for years how Elaine was having a major impact on the lives of her clients. After working for fifteen years at HP, Scott saw that his true passion was also to help people achieve their goals. He joined Elaine so that together they could have a bigger impact on the lives of more families. Together, they built one of the largest teams at their firm.

When Elaine and Scott started their new firm in 2018, they wanted to create a firm that was different from other financial firms, building on their decades of experience. They wanted their clients to see them as *Partners in Your Financial Journey®*. Scott designed the new office for Financial Journey Partners to create the ideal space that is comfortable and inviting for clients to plan and implement their goals and dreams. Financial Journey Partners has an experienced team to provide a high level of service for our clients.

Elaine and Scott are excited every day to come to work and help their clients reach their goals and *Enjoy the Journey* along the way. Elaine and Scott feel blessed to have in their lives so many wonderful people that are clients and friends, and for them, this is how they *Enjoy the Journey*.

This book is designed to be practical and inspirational and help you make smart decisions as you *Enjoy the Journey*. Start your journey today!

www.ingramcontent.com/pod-product-compliance
Ingram Content Group UK Ltd.
Pitfield, Milton Keynes, MK11 3LW, UK
UKHW022030041026
15591UKWH00012B/594

9 798989 205677